Classic Hollywood Stars

Portraits & Quotes

Mike Oldham

Schiffer Publishing Ltd

4880 Lower Valley Road, Atglen, Pa 19310

Other Schiffer Books by Mike Oldham:
Greetings from Beverly Hills
More Hollywood Homes

Schiffer Books are available at special discounts for bulk purchases for sales promotions or premiums. Special editions, including personalized covers, corporate imprints, and excerpts can be created in large quantities for special needs. For more information contact the publisher:

Published by Schiffer Publishing Ltd.
4880 Lower Valley Road
Atglen, PA 19310
Phone: (610) 593-1777; Fax: (610) 593-2002
E-mail: Info@schifferbooks.com

For the largest selection of fine reference books on this and related subjects, please visit our web site at **www.schifferbooks.com**
We are always looking for people to write books on new and related subjects. If you have an idea for a book please contact us at the above address.

This book may be purchased from the publisher.
Include $5.00 for shipping.
Please try your bookstore first.
You may write for a free catalog.

In Europe, Schiffer books are distributed by
Bushwood Books
6 Marksbury Ave.
Kew Gardens
Surrey TW9 4JF England
Phone: 44 (0) 20 8392-8585; Fax: 44 (0) 20 8392-9876
E-mail: info@bushwoodbooks.co.uk
Website: www.bushwoodbooks.co.uk

Free postage in the U.K., Europe; air mail at cost.

Designed by RoS
Type set in Isadora/ Aldine721 BT

ISBN: 978-0-7643-3050-6

Printed in China

Dedication

To
Kelley and Steve Wright
Kevie and Doug Marsden
These parents single-handedly started an entire new era in my family. Where would the family be without them and their kids? Yet I never tell them this . . . (And thank goodness they are fantastic parents!)

Acknowledgments

I appreciate that Tina Skinner, of Schiffer Publishing, became enthusiastic about this book after I completed *More Hollywood Homes*.

Judy Artunian did me a big favor without knowing it. She told me to skip the singer Fabian when doing the book. Judy told me this without knowing I had already purchased a postcard of Fabian. The way she told me not to include him told me how Fabian was perceived during his heyday. Hence, Judy is responsible for part of a line in my introduction ("and yes, Fabian"). Judy also provided fifty quotes for the book. I don't want to tell you which ones are hers because they're better than mine! (*Thanks Judy! Oh, and sorry, Judy, about putting Fabian in the book!*)

I struggled to describe actor Troy Donahue's appearance, so I phoned Sherrie Oldham, my mom, who said, "Troy Donahue has boyish looks." Problem solved. (*Thanks Mom!*)

Contents

Introduction

This book was created to display the postcards of actors, actresses, singers, and entertainers. The book is also filled with rare quotes of the stars. Many of the quotes cannot be found in other biographies, as they were culled from gumshoe research.

Something happens when you gaze upon a vintage postcard featuring a star or two. This book was created to bring that "something" to people other than postcard collectors. I wrote many long sentences that headed in all directions while attempting to define that "something." The time was not wasted, for it gave me the answer: that "something" can only be defined by an individual viewing the postcards. Who can put into words the thoughts and feelings that materialize when gazing at a postcard of Dolores Del Rio or Billie Dove or John Gilbert?

Stars have many sides to their personalities that can often get lost, due to one film, one song, or one television show. A postcard can display Anthony Perkins as a classy Hollywood star of a bye-gone era. This is contrasted with the overly repeated image of him as a spooky guy running a roadside motel. A card can remind us of the Diana Shore of earlier days, long before her daytime television persona. Gloria Swanson may have been destined to play Norma Desmond, but she began in films as a silent player.

Classic Hollywood Stars is about bringing things back. Count Basie, Tommy Sands, and yes, Fabian, where have you gone? The postcard images and printed thoughts bring them back for us to know and cherish.

The classic stars of the past continue to age well, like a good wine. Today's stars will create a vintage look of their own, in the years to come. But it will be a different one than those of the stars of the 1920s through the 1950s.

Mike Oldham

Notes on Postcard Collecting

This book is only a tease of an introduction to collecting postcards of entertainers. There is an unknown amount—perhaps tens of thousands—of star postcards one can ultimately collect. There are theater stars, movie stars, singers, comedians, and general entertainers that have been captured in postcards.

To hunt them down is half the fun of creating a collection. Postcard shows feature tables of various dealers who offer postcards for sale. One can bid in online auctions to start a collection. In the end, if there is desire to collect the star postcards, a way will be found to find them.

Finally, postcard collecting is actually not a cheap exercise. Once the collecting bug is caught, a collector can be found paying around $15 per card and up for their favorite movie star or singer.

MAURICE CHEVALIER AND ANN DVORAK
IN "THE WAY TO LOVE"

June Allyson
(1917–2006)
Actress

Born in New York, actress June Allyson would become a leading lady on the screen in the 1940s. In the 1944 film, *Two Girls and a Sailor*, Allyson starred with Gloria DeHaven, playing the part of her sister. In 1945, Allyson would marry a leading man, actor Dick Powell. The famous Hollywood couple would stay together until Powell's death in 1963. Allyson would die in California in 2006.

"I'm really a homely type."
—June Allyson

Pier Angeli

(1932–1971)
Actress

Pier Angeli

WARNER BROS

Pier
Angeli
Value
of card:
$10-12

Pier Angeli was a wiry, pretty actress who became a film star in the 1950s. She was born in Italy and that would be where she first made it onto the screen. The 1951 film, *Teresa*, won her good notices. She would go on to star in films with the likes of actors Gene Kelly and Paul Newman. In 1971, Hollywood was shocked to learn that Angeli had overdosed on pills in her home in Beverly Hills, California.

> *"When my sister came into the lunchroom at the studio they called her Pocahontas, because she had an Indian headdress. They call me Moose, though not because I look like one of those big animals, but on account of our little dog called Moose."*
> —Pier Angeli, whose sister is actress Marisa Pavan

Annabella

Annabella
(1909–1996)
Actress

Annabella was born in France in 1909 and would become a film star there the 1930s. In the late 1930s she was making films in Hollywood. Annabella starred in the 1937 film called *Under the Red Robe*. Her screen achievements may be overshadowed by her marriage to actor Tyrone Power in 1939. The couple would divorce by the close of the 1940s. Annabella would never marry again.

"It is not always good to be a film star in America. It is like being a goldfish in a bowl. They must know what I eat, what I think, they even want to know whom I love—and that I tell no one."

—Annabella, who started her film career in her native France

Louis Armstrong

(1901–1971)
Musician

Louis
Armstrong

PARAMOUNT

Louis Armstrong was born in a city known for music, New Orleans. Armstrong would become known for playing music as a trumpeter. Besides his musical talent, the man was famous for his smile and upbeat persona. Armstrong was also well known as a vocalist. He made good use of his raspy voice in the hit record, "What a Wonderful World" (1968).

Louis Armstrong Value of card: $7-9

"The horns wear out but not me . . . Retirement? Where I come from they don't know what that word is."

—Louis Armstrong, at age sixty-one

15

Fred Astaire

(1899–1987)
Actor

Fred
Astaire
Value
of card:
$10-12

Fred Astaire

"Ross" Verlag

A 1190/1

Reproduction verboten

Actor Fred Astaire danced with actress Ginger Rogers in the 1933 film, *Flying Down to Rio*. The two would dance together in many films to come making them Hollywood's most-famous dancing couple. *Top Hat* (1935) and *Swing Time* (1936) are among the more memorable films Astaire would dance in. The Actor signed a lucrative contract with RKO Radio Pictures in the mid-1930s.

> *"I have never thought of myself as spic and span or all duded out—just as some one who wants to be comfortable and satisfy his own taste."*
> —Fred Astaire

Mary Astor

(1906–1987)
Actress

Mary Astor

"Ross" Verlag

Reproduction verboten

Actress Mary Astor had a film career that spanned over four decades. Her Hollywood days began in the silent-film era of the early 1920s and ended in the mid-1960s. She starred with actor Humphrey Bogart in the classic film of 1939 called *The Maltese Falcon*. Astor played the role of Marmee in *Little Women* (1949). Television would keep Astor busy in the 1950s and early 1960s.

> "Several times I've thought the movies were ready to call it quits with me; but here I am at the same old game . . . One of the reasons I've stayed the course is because I haven't cared whether I kept in the race or not."
> —Mary Astor

Frankie
Avalon

Frankie Avalon

(1939–)
Singer

Frankie Avalon was still a teenager when he became a famous singer and teen idol. Songs "Venus" and "Why" were both top Billboard hits in 1959. Plenty of hit records followed and soon Avalon branched out into films. Avalon played Smitty in a film that both starred and was directed by actor John Wayne called *The Alamo* in 1960.

> *"I think rock 'n' roll is great for this generation. I think it gives a happy feeling to music. We don't dress like they did back in the 40s. Well, this is the same thing."*
> —Frankie Avalon, 1960

George Bancroft

(1882–1956)
Actor

George
Bancroft
Value
of card:
$7-9

Born in Philadelphia, George Bancroft was a tough-guy actor in the late 1920s. He starred in the 1927 film, *Underworld*. He had a memorable film to his credit in 1936 called *Mr. Deeds Goes to Town*. Late in his career he was a familiar character actor. Bancroft died in 1956 in Santa Monica, California where he had a house on the beach.

"Life has been just one bed of roses for me. I never had to struggle or starve, everything always fell just right for me. People like me and just do things for me."
—George Bancroft

5086/1
Ross-Verlag

Reproduction verboten.

Vilma Banky

Vilma Banky

(1898–1991)
Actress

Silent-film actress Vilma Banky starred in *Son of the Sheik* (1926) and *Two Lovers* (1928). The screen career of the actress did not last long after the end of the silent-film era. She was done with Hollywood by the early 1930s. In 1927, Banky married another silent star, actor Rod La Roque. They would remain married until La Roque's death in 1969.

"Do not call me anudder Mary Peekfard. I am jus Vilma Banky of Budapest. An' it is Mees Banky. I am not married."
—Vilma Banky, who had been called "Europe's Mary Pickford," upon arriving in Los Angeles from Budapest in 1925 and admitting she speaks "no Engleesh"

John Barrymore

(1882–1942)
Actor

5386
United Artists
Verleih: Super-Film

John Barrymore

„Iris"-Verlag

John Barrymore was a famous stage and film actor. He was a leading man beginning in the silent-film era. Barrymore was nicknamed "The Great Profile." *The Sea Beast* (1926) and *Grand Hotel* (1932) are among his well-known films. In the late 1920s, Barrymore married actress Dolores Costello. The actors would split in the mid-1930s. Barrymore was known for having a humorous outlook on life even during hard financial times that he had experienced beginning in the 1930s.

John Barrymore Value of card: $8-10

> *"Acting is not an art. It's a junk pile of all the arts. But in [sic] behalf of my scavenger profession I'll make this boast. An actor is much better off than a human being. He isn't stuck with the paltry fellow he is. He can always act his better and non-existent self."*
> —John Barrymore

21

Richard Barthelmess

498/1

Iris Verlag

Richard Barthelmess

Beßina
3136/1

„Ross" Verlag

Richard Barthelmess

(1895–1963)
Actor

Born in New York, silent-star actor Richard Barthelmess became famous with such films as *Way Down East* (1920). The film co-starred his friend, actress Lillian Gish. Barthelmess starred in the film, *The Dawn Patrol* (1930). He worked with legendary silent-film director D.W. Griffith. Barthelmess died wealthy on Long Island.

"To this day I have an aversion to custard pies, due to my first experience in pictures. You see, I started in slapstick comedy at the princely salary of twenty-five dollars a week and my main part was to serve as a target for culinary products."
—Richard Barthelmess, 1923

COURTESY OF
MUSIC CORPORATION OF AMERICA

Count Basie

(1904–1984)
Bandleader/Musician

Musical artist Count Basie was born in New Jersey in 1904. The pianist came to fame out of the swing era of jazz and the big band sound of the 1930s. His band he put together in the mid-1930s eventually came to be known as the Count Basie Orchestra. "Taxi War Dance" (1939) was one of the celebrated pieces of the band. Basie's health began to decline in the 1970s. He died in Florida in 1984.

"I wanted to be called 'Buck' or 'Hoot' or even 'Arkansas Fats."
—Count Basie, who admitted he hated the name "Count" that stuck with him after a radio announcer tagged him with it

Count Basie
Value of
card: $5-7

Constance Bennett

Constance Bennett

Constance Bennett

(1904–1965)
Actress

Reproduction verboten

„Ross" Verlag

Constance
Bennett
Value
of card:
$10-12

Born in New York, Constance Bennett was said to be the highest paid actress in Hollywood at one point in the early 1930s. She once admitted to a reporter that she wanted to become rich. Wealth would bring her independence she said. Bennett made money from films like *What Price Hollywood* (1932) and *Topper* (1937). Her sisters were actresses Joan and Barbara Bennett.

> *"Among the Hollywood detestables, even I was no match for Constance, who could sit across from me at the dinner table at Marion Davies's beach house and never acknowledge my existence with so much as an icy nod."*
> —Actress Louise Brooks

Joan Bennett

118   *Joan Bennett*

Joan Bennett
Value of card:
$10-12

Joan
Bennett
Value
of card:
$8-10

Joan Bennett

(1910–1990)
Actress

Joan Bennett starred in the classic movie called *Little Women* (1933). By the late 1930s, the actress was earning seven-thousand dollars per week. Another memorable one of Bennett's films was the 1944 movie called *The Woman in the Window*. She did not have much success at marriage. Bennett collected four husbands before dying in 1990.

> *"There was a limit, perhaps, to what you could say to her. I don't think she was an intellectual, and I certainly didn't talk to her about books or anything like that—but I always felt that she was very interested in what I was doing."*

—Timothy Anderson, grandson of Joan Bennett

Jack
Benny
Value
of card:
$5-7

Jack Benny
Value
of card:
$10-12

Jack Benny

(1894–1974)
Comedian/Actor

Comedian Jack Benny became hugely famous through radio and television. His popular radio show was called *The Jack Benny Show* (1932–1955). Benny had television success with "The Jack Benny Program" (1950–1965). These shows combined made Benny an entertainment institution with American audiences. The comedian also acted in films such as *To Be or Not to Be* (1942). Benny had homes in the California cities of Beverly Hills and Palm Springs.

> *"I went to see one of those X-rated pictures the other night, and I couldn't believe my eyes. So I stayed to see it a second time."*
> —Jack Benny

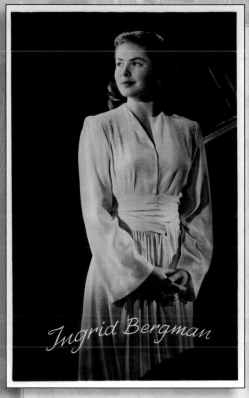

Ingrid Bergman

INGRID BERGMAN

Ingrid Bergman
Value of card:
$10-12

Ingrid
Bergman
Value of
card: $7-9

Ingrid Bergman

(1915–1982)
Actress

Born in Sweden, actress Ingrid Bergman came to the America in the 1930s to make pictures for producer David O'Selznick. Her first movie for him would be the 1939 film called *Intermezzo: A Love Story*. She would go on to make the classics, *Casablanca* (1942) and *For Whom the Bell Tolls* (1943). One of Bergman's daughters is actress Isabella Rossellini.

"I did not come to Hollywood in the first place because there were fame, riches, and glamour to be gained here. I came here because this is a place where pictures are made, many of them very excellent, and I felt that here was opportunity for the actress."
—Ingrid Bergman

D. 216

ANN BLYTH AND CARL ESMOND
in "The World in his Arms"

UNIVERSAL INTERN

Ann
Blyth
and Carl
Esmond
Value
of card:
$10-12

Ann Blyth

(1928–)
Actress

Ann Blyth's striking beauty served her well in Hollywood. Less known about the star is that she worked professionally as a singer before becoming an actress. Playing the role of Joan Crawford's daughter in the 1945 film, *Mildred Pierce*, would make her famous. Blyth's other movie credits include starring roles in the *Swell Guy* (1946) and *Killer McCoy* (1947).

> *"I wanted to be a singer, but chance put me in a Broadway play. I was eating lunch at school one day when Herman Shumlin, the producer, came into the room and looked over a group of us girls. The next day Mr. Shumlin sent for me. I read for him, and got the daughter's part in Watch on the Rhine."*
> —Ann Blyth

Humphrey Bogart

(1899–1957)
Actor

Humphrey Bogart was born in New York, New York in 1899. Besides acting a small part in a 1920 film, he started his film career with the movie called *Up the River* (1930). Previously he had acted on stage. It is difficult to find a Bogart movie that is not enjoyable to watch. He banked many classic films during his career. *The Maltese Falcon* (1941) and *The Treasure of the Sierra Madre* (1948) were two of them. He had a famous wife in actress Lauren Bacall. The two married in 1945. Bogart and Bacall stayed together until his death in 1957.

> *"Bogart, go back to Broadway and stay there. We've shot you from every possible angle and there isn't a single photogenic feature about you."*
> —Producer Harry Cohn to Humphrey Bogart, as he was trying to gain a foothold in Hollywood

Humphrey Bogart Value of card: $12-14

CLARA BOW   348

Clara Bow

(1907–1965)
Actress

Clara Bow became known as the "It Girl" after starring in the film, *It* (1928). This became the signature film of the Brooklyn-born actress. Bow had movie success before *It* with such films as *The Plastic Age* (1925) and *Mantrap* (1926). Her stardom dimmed in the sound era of movies and by the early 1930s Bow's film career was over. Bow struggled with metal illness in her later years of life.

> *"Then, maybe in five years, when I'm 25, I'll quit.*
> *I don't want to just dwindle away, but stop when I'm*
> *going good. And I won't 'come back'—ever."*
> —Clara Bow

William Boyd

(1895–1972)
Actor

William Boyd

Verlag „Ross" Berlin SW 66.

William Boyd and Hopalong Cassidy are nearly synonymous names to film fans of actor Boyd. Playing the western character Hopalong Cassidy in numerous films made Boyd wealthy. Early Hopalong Cassidy films included *Heart of the West* (1936) and *Borderland* (1937). Even after retiring to Palm Desert, California, Boyd was both proud and protective of the Hopalong Cassidy character's image.

William Boyd Value of card: $10-12

"I'm afraid that an interview is quite impossible. I haven't given one in years. And I don't want any pictures taken. I'm not the man people remember as Hopalong Cassidy. They'd be shocked at the difference. I don't want to tamper with their memories . . . Besides, I don't have anything interesting to tell. There's nothing new. I haven't done anything professional since 1953; my last public appearance was in 1959. I'm out of the picture now. Who'd be interested in reading about somebody in retirement? . . . I don't want to hash over the past again. It's done, and I want to leave the record as it is. I'm too old for this kind of thing."

—William Boyd, talking to a reporter in 1969

MARLON BRANDO
METRO GOLDWYN MAYER
510

Marlon Brando
(1924–2004)
Actor

Marlon
Brando
Value
of card:
$10-12

Marlon Brando was born in Nebraska in 1924. He starred in many classic films during his long Hollywood acting career. *A Streetcar Named Desire* (1951) and *On the Waterfront* (1954) are a couple of classic Brando films. Off screen, the actor was known as an eccentric person. Brando was friends with another eccentric entertainer, pop star Michael Jackson.

> *"When I'm reading a book, I don't need a first edition to enjoy it. A dollar copy is good enough so long as the words are there."*
> —Marlon Brando

BETTY BRONSON.

1701/1

Betty Bronson

Verlag „Ross" Berlin SW 68.

Betty Bronson
Value of card:
$12-14

Betty
Bronson
Value
of card:
$12-14

Betty Bronson

(1906–1971)
Actress

Betty Bronson was an extremely popular actress in the mid-1920s. Her fame was nearly solely due to the film, *Peter Pan* (1924). In the silent picture, Bronson played the title role of Peter Pan. Surprisingly, Bronson would be all but finished as a screen actress by the end of the 1930s.

"Yes, I always play 'nice girls' and I am not yearning to play tough ones—quite content to say in character, thank you. Of course, I like being different kinds of nice girls, but I think I have been rather lucky in that. Funny, but I feel as if I have been in pictures forever…

"I would like to play one good stage role if I get the chance, so that I could take up the stage when I am quite old, about 30, you know. And the talkies are good training for that, don't you think?"

—Betty Bronson

Billie Burke

(1884–1970)
Actress

Billie
Burke
Value
of card:
$10-12

Billie Burke was born to an entertainment family. The actress would work on the stage in London as a young lady. Burke made it to the Broadway stage before eventually turning to film work. Today, Burke's career is all but forgotten with the exception of her role as Good Witch Glenda in the film, *The Wizard of Oz* (1939). Today's younger fans of the movie are not likely to know the name of the actress playing Glenda. Burke called the role her favorite.

> *"Every now and then when I start being a little vague in a crisis, my child says, 'See here, mother, you can't do that. You're not one of those woman you play on the screen. They can step aside from reality, but you can't!'"*

—Billie Burke, 1937

Francis X. Bushman and Ramon Novarro
Value of card: $10-12

Francis X. Bushman   Ben Hur   Ramon Novarro

"Iris Verlag"

Francis X. Bushman

(1883–1966)
Actor

Francis X. Bushman had a name that was easy to remember. But today the actor is forgotten despite a movie career that lasted over five decades. *Bill Bumper's Bargain* (1911) and *Daydream of a Photoplay Artist* (1912) were among the films he appeared in during his first years as a screen actor. Bushman starred with Ramon Novarro in the 1925 film, *Ben-Hur: A Tale of the Christ*. The actor not only had a long acting career but a long life as well. Bushman was born in Maryland in 1883 and died in 1966.

Ramon Novarro

(1899–1968)
Actor

Mexico-born Ramon Novarro put in several years as a film extra before he became a star in the early 1920s. The 1922 film, *The Prisoner of Zenda*, was his breakout movie. Today, Novarro is most remembered for starring in *Ben-Hur: A Tale of the Christ* (1925). Tragedy struck in 1968 when Novarro was brutally murdered in his home in the Hollywood Hills area of California.

"Great pictures? There were none. I've never liked anything I've done: I always thought what it could have been, but wasn't."
—Ramon Novarro, 1949

James Cagney

(1899–1986)
Actor

JAMES CAGNEY

James Cagney began his film acting in the 1930s. During his career he would star in many memorable films such as *The Public Enemy* (1931) and *Yankee Doodle Dandy* (1942). Cagney was known as a versatile actor who could play a tough guy or a romantic suitor. The actor spent his retirement years on a Martha's Vineyard farm he owned.

"The men I'm supposed to sock in my films get scared sometimes. An actor walked out of my last picture when he heard I had to beat him up."
—James Cagney, 1936

EDDIE CANTOR   UNITED ARTISTS

Eddie Cantor and Tom Breneman

Eddie Cantor
Value of card:
$6-8

Eddie
Cantor
and Tom
Brene-
man
Value
of card:
$5-7

Eddie Cantor

(1892–1964)
Actor

Eddie Cantor entertained on the stage, radio, and the silver screen. He was a waiter and entertainer in a saloon as a teenager. Cantor the actor would star in the films, *Whoopee* (1930) and *Kid Millions* (1934). Shortly before he died in 1964 he expressed disappointment with the new crop of entertainers. "I am disturbed by the younger generation in show business, however," said Cantor in 1963. "They seem to think first of capital gains and bank accounts in Switzerland." He stayed married to his wife, Ida, for nearly fifty years until her death in the early 1960s.

"I never had an ambition higher than to make people laugh. It's the easiest thing in the world to make 'em cry."
—Eddie Cantor

Lon Chaney

Metro-Goldwyn-Film.

879

Lon Chaney

„Iris" Verlag

Lon Chaney

(1883–1930)
Actor

Lon Chaney Value of card: $13-15

Lon Chaney was an actor who pioneered many movie make-up techniques. He would become known as "The Man of a Thousand Faces." His face appeared in many classic silent pictures such as *The Phantom of the Opera* (1925) and *Laugh Clown, Laugh* (1928). Chaney was Quasimodo in the 1923 film, *The Hunchback of Notre Dame*. Beverly Hills was Chaney's home when he died wealthy at the age of forty-seven.

"I am perhaps the only screen actor who can walk down the street and not be recognized."
—Lon Chaney, who was known as "The Man of a Thousand Faces"

61   CHARLIE CHAPLIN dit CHARLOT

UNITED ARTISTS
A.N PARIS

Charles Chaplin

(1889–1977)
Actor

Charles Chaplin Value of card: $18-20

Charles Chaplin grew up poor in England. He told his children that he himself was lucky to get an orange for Christmas as a child. The actor would tell his kids such things before allowing them to open their many presents under their Christmas tree each year. Chaplin would become very rich as a silent-screen acting legend. *The Kid* (1921) and *The Gold Rush* (1925) were among his many successful films in the 1920s. He had success in the 1930s with the films, *City Lights* (1931) and *Modern Times* (1936). Chaplin did more than act in films. The comic genius produced and directed most of his movies. Chaplin lived in a mansion he had built in Beverly Hills for most of his Hollywood years.

> *"There was a strong element of the merchant in me. I was continuously preoccupied with business schemes. I would look at empty shops, speculating as to what profitable businesses I could make of them, ranging from fish and chips to grocery shops."*

—Charles Chaplin, on his childhood in England

CYD CHARISSE

METRO GOLDWYN MAYER

516

Cyd Charisse

(1921– 2008)
Actress

Cyd
Charisse
Value
of card:
$10-12

Cyd Charisse began training as a dancer early in her life. She took ballet lessons as a kid. Charisse would dance with no less than actor/dancer Fred Astaire in the films *Ziegfeld Follies* and *The Band Wagon* (1953). She married singer Tony Martin in 1948.

"Dancing is my first love, really. On the other hand, I don't like to just dance. I enjoy an acting part. It's like a vacation for me. Dancing is very hard work, which most people overlook."

—Cyd Charisse, who danced her way into movie fame

Chubby Checker

(1941–)
Singer

Chubby Checker

Singer Chubby Checker was born in Spring Gulley, South Carolina, in 1941. His birth name was Ernest Evans. Checker recorded "The Twist" in 1959, but it did not become a hit record until the summer of 1960. He had another hit on the charts in the early 1960s with "Pony Time" (1961). Checker had many more hit records that followed.

Chubby Checker Value of card: $10-12

"In two minutes and 42 seconds, we changed the way people danced. [The Twist] is putting out a cigarette with both feet. We're looking stupid trying to look sexy."
—Chubby Checker, on his hit song, "The Twist" (1959), and the Twist dance craze that followed

41

Maurice Chevalier

„Ross" Verlag   Reproduction verboten

Maurice
Chevalier

(1888–1972)
Actor

Maurice Chevalier started film acting in his native country of France. He did short films such as *Par habitude* (1911). Chevalier also worked on stage in Europe before making it to Hollywood in the late 1920s. Chevalier was a singing talent and his voice was put to work in the film, *The Love Parade* (1929). The musical co-starred actress Jeanette MacDonald. Chevalier would work with MacDonald again in *Love Me Tonight* (1932). Off screen, Chevalier did not get along with MacDonald.

> *"If I had my life to live all over again—and I would not want to—I would take love more seriously than I was taught to take it as a kid. I would not throw myself in every corner with any girl I meet. For the rest, I feel I've done the best I could, considering I was born to be a workingman."*
> —Maurice Chevalier at age seventy

MAURICE CHEVALIER AND ANN DVORAK IN "THE WAY TO LOVE"

PARAMOUNT

Ann Dvorak

(1912–1979)
Actress

Born into a Hollywood family, Ann Dvorak began her film career as a child actor in silent films. Grown up, she would play opposite actor Spencer Tracy in the 1932 film, *Sky Devils*. Dvorak would star in *The Strange Love of Molly Louvain* (1932). Her last films were released in the early 1950s. Dvorak died in Honolulu, Hawaii in 1979.

"I believe you can do anything in the world, if you really want to do it hard enough. It isn't even intelligence perhaps. It's a sense of values."
—Ann Dvorak

Maurice
Chevalier
and Ann
Dvorak
Value
of card:
$10-12

Nat "King" Cole

Nat "King" Cole

(1919–1965)
Singer

Nat
"King"
Cole
Value
of card:
$6-8

    Nat King Cole was born in Montgomery, Alabama in 1919. The singer formed his famous band called King Cole Trio in the late 1930s. The band would tour extensively. One of Cole's hit songs was "Mona Lisa" (1950). His second marriage was to big-band singer Maria Cole in the late 1940s. One of their children is singer Natalie Cole.

> *"I never looked at the audience, even after years of singing. I was too scared."*
> —Nat King Cole

Ronald Colman

Ronald Colman

(1891–1958)
Actor

Born in England, actor Ronald Colman starred in a silent film made in the United Kingdom called *A Son of David* (1920). He would soon come to America and do acting on the Broadway stage. Colman would take his talents to Hollywood. He starred in the 1925 film called *The Dark Angel*. When talking pictures arrived, Coleman did not miss a beat in his screen career. *The Unholy Garden* (1931) was among Coleman's first talkies.

"Oh, ten years hence I'll still be living in California, and probably talking about the good old days in motion pictures."
—Ronald Colman, 1935

Ronald Colman
Value
of card:
$10-12

BETTY COMPSON

Betty Compson

(1897–1974)
Actress

Actress Betty Compson was a silent-film star. *Paths to Paradise* (1925) and *The Docks of New York* (1928) are a couple of her memorable films. In the mid-1920s, Compson married actor, producer, and director James Cruze. The marriage did not last past 1930.

> *"Stars who insist upon knowing before they agree to play roles whether or not they can suitably enact them are the only ones who can survive as box office successes."*
>
> —Betty Compson

Chuck Connors

(1921–1992)
Actor

Chuck Connors played with baseballs and basketballs as a professional before turning to acting. He played with a rifle when he starred in the television series, "The Rifleman" (1958–1963). Connors enjoyed Palm Springs, California so much he bought a home there in the 1960s.

Chuck
Connors
Value of
card: $7-9

> *"Now, they ask me why another half-hour series? Why television when movies are available? Why an advertising medium? In order to work in this profession you have to accept what is. It's not a question of compromising to an advertising medium—you have to adjust to it.*
>
> *"If you really want true creative art, go to the public library and get Shakespeare. Then go to Griffith Park and play it! But you won't do it. You'll want an audience and you'll want them to pay to see you."*
>
> —Chuck Connors, in a 1965 interview just before the premier of his television series, "Branded" (1965–1966)

Jackie Coogan

Verlag „Ross" Berlin SW 68.

Jackie Coogan
(1914–1984)
Actor

As a child, actor Jackie Coogan became a silent-film sensation when he starred in actor Charles Chaplin's film, *The Kid* (1921). Coogan is also remembered for being forced to file suit against his parents in the 1930s. His suit was an effort to recover his film earnings they held. Coogan ended up gaining only a fraction of the earnings back from his parents. Coogan was born and raised in Los Angeles, California.

> *"My town's destroyed. I was born here. It's terrible to see it go to pot. Pittsburgh, where you once couldn't wear a shirt for more than an hour, is a lot cleaner than Hollywood."*
> —Jackie Coogan, 1969

GARY COOPER   PARAMOUNT PICTURES

Gary Cooper

Gary Cooper

(1901–1961)
Actor

Gary Cooper became a star after he played a bit part in the 1927 film, *Wings*. The actor known for both his great looks and acting talent would go on to make heartwarming films like *The Pride of the Yankees* (1942). Cooper was known as being tightfisted with the money he banked from his film career.

"When he wasn't before the cameras he sat crosslegged whittling on such lumber as was available."

—Actress Tallulah Bankhead speaking of Gary Cooper's behavior on a movie set

MISS GLADYS COOPER.

11861 W ROTARY PHOTO. E.C.

PHOTOGRAPH BY
FOULSHAM & BANFIELD, LTD
42, OLD BOND ST., W

Gladys
Cooper
Value
of card:
$10-12

Gladys Cooper

(1888–1971)
Actress

England-born actress Gladys Cooper was good at playing snobbish-character roles. As an actress, her "bread and butter" was the stage. Cooper started her theater work as a teenager. But she would work in Hollywood. Cooper played the role of Mrs. Hamilton in the 1947 film, *The Bishop's Wife*.

"She had this terrible disadvantage when she started out. She was quite the most beautiful actress in London."
—Director George Cukor on Gladys Cooper

Jackie Cooper

(1922–)
Actor

JACKIE COOPER   PARAMOUNT

Jackie
Cooper
Value
of card:
$7-9

Jackie Cooper was a child star in Hollywood. From 1929 through 1931, the actor played one of The Little Rascals for the *Our Gang* (1922–1944) series. Cooper would co-star with actor Wallace Beery in the 1931 film, *The Champ*. Television has keep Cooper busy in more recent decades.

> *"Hollywood is no place to learn to act. I was just*
> *a kid who could take direction. Most child actors are.*
> *The directors do the work, The Taurogs, The McLeods,*
> *the Boleslawkis. You just do what they tell you."*
> —Jackie Cooper

51

Dolores
Costello

75-B

DOLORES COSTELLO
(Warner Bros. et Vitaphone Pictures)

Dolores
Costello
Value
of card:
$10-12

Dolores Costello
Value of card:
$13-15

Dolores Costello

(1903–1979)
Actress

Actress Dolores Costello was known as the "Goddess of the Silent Screen." She began her acting career as a child and appeared in many silent films in the early days of movie making. Costello appeared in *The Child Crusoes* (1911) and *The Meeting of the Ways* (1912). She continued film making as an adult and co-starred with actor John Barrymore in the 1926 film, *The Sea Beast*. Costello would marry Barrymore in 1928. Costello's skin was too delicate for the studio makeup and she was out of pictures by the early 1940s.

"She was too beautiful for words, but not for arguments."
—Actor John Barrymore on his third wife, Dolores Costello, around the time of their divorce in 1935

JOAN CRAWFORD

855

Joan Crawford

Joan Crawford

(1905–1977)
Actress

Actress Joan Crawford was first a star in the silent-film era of the 1920s. But she would excel as well with sound pictures such as *Strange Cargo* (1940) and *Mildred Pierce* (1945). Some say the actress was distant and hard to gauge off screen. Crawford's daughter, Christina, wrote a stinging book called *Mommie Dearest: A True Story.* It portrayed Crawford as a not-so-good parent. The book was published after Crawford's death and has deeply damaged the public memory of her. Crawford died in 1977.

"I have respect for my body and try to take care of it. I eat well but wisely. I have trained myself to stay away from foods that aren't good for me. I used to be tempted like anyone else by a rich cake or beautiful candy, but I've learned that when I eat a lot of sweets and starches I don't feel as well.

"Is there more fun in the world than feeling well and looking your best?"

—Joan Crawford, 1952

Curtis

(1925–)
Actor

Tony
Curtis
Value
of card:
$6-8

Born in New York, Tony Curtis is a versatile actor. His films like *The Sweet Smell of Success* (1957) and *Some Like It Hot* (1959) proved this out. Curtis married actress Janet Leigh in the early 1950s. The marriage would not last past the early 1960s.

> *"I guess I've still got some of that old live-it-up left in me. I'm buying a Rolls Royce convertible. Going the whole route, you might say."*
> —Tony Curtis, 1959

Lili Damita

(1904–1994)
Actress

Lily Damita

The film career of actress Lili Damita began in France in the early 1920s. Before it ended in the 1930s, she would do some Hollywood films. Damita starred in the film, *The Match King* (1932). Today, Damita is remembered not for her films, but for being Errol Flynn's first wife. The couple married in the mid-1930s and divorced in the early 1940s. Damita died in Florida in 1994.

> "*I nevair knew a wedding she could be so tres grande! She was heavenly.*"
> —Lili Damita, a native of France, describing her then-recent 1935 wedding to actor Errol Flynn while struggling with English

Lili Damita (aka Lily Damita) Value of card: $12-14

Bebe Daniels

BEBE DANIELS

Bebe Daniels
Value of card:
$10-12

Bebe
Daniels
Value
of card:
$10-12

Bebe Daniels

(1901–1971)
Actress

Silent-star actress Bebe Daniels first appeared in films as a child. As an adult, she would star in the films, *Monsieur Beaucaire* (1924) and *Music Is Magic* (1935). Daniels married actor Ben Lyon in 1930.

> *"My work comes nearest my heart. I love it and am interested in it above everything. I can't take anything else really seriously, unless it is building and decorating houses and selling them in my vacation times. I can't even enjoy holidays. I itch to be back at work again. And I play bridge for recreation, which is less dangerous than tinkering with romance."*
> —Bebe Daniels, 1927

Marion Davies
(1897–1961)
Actress

1026

Ⓒ

MARION DAVIES

Marion
Davies
Value of
card: $6-8

As an actress, blond-haired Marion Davies was best in comedy roles. *The Patsy* (1928) demonstrated her comic talents. Today, the actress is remembered less for her acting. Davies is best remembered for having a long-term romance with publisher William Randolph Hearst while he remained married. Davies died wealthy in 1961.

"I was handicapped because I stuttered. Somebody told me I should put a pebble in my mouth to cure my stuttering. That practice goes back to the Grecian period. Well, I tried it, and during a scene I swallowed the pebble. That was the end of that."
—Marion Davies, 1954

James Dean
in
"... denn sie wissen nicht, was sie tun"

James
Dean

WARNER BROS

James
Dean
Value
of card:
$13-15

James Dean
Value of card:
$13-15

James Dean

(1931–1955)
Actor

James Dean is known for playing rebellious characters on the screen. The actor is also known for dying in a tragic car accident that shocked Hollywood in 1955. Dean's acting efforts include the 1955 film, *Rebel Without a Cause.*

> *"I'm a serious-minded and intense little devil—terribly gauche . . . and so tense I don't see how people stay in the same room with me. I know I wouldn't tolerate myself!"*
> —James Dean

Sandra Dee

(1942–2005)
Actress

Sandra
Dee
Value of
card: $4-6

Blond-haired Sandra Dee is famous for starring in the 1959 film, *Imitation of Life*. She is also known for her marriage to singer Bobby Darin in 1960. The couple would do films together. By the close of the 1960s, Dee would be divorced from Darin and out of work in Hollywood. She never remarried.

"Your mother showed you the beauty of life; with me you'll see the seamy side."
—Singer Bobby Darin to his bride Sandra Dee in 1960

GLORIA DE HAVEN

Gloria De
Haven
Value
of card:
$10-12

Gloria DeHaven
Value of card:
$10-12

Gloria DeHaven

(1925–)
Actress

A California native, actress Gloria DeHaven worked in musical films. One of her earliest films was *Broadway Rhythm* (1944). DeHaven was in the 1950 movie, *Three Little Words*. The actress has done a lot of stage and television work in her long career.

"I became unhappy under my Fox contract and decided to try the road. It's quite an experience, pays well, but it's wonderful to be able to be able to break up the club routine with a picture commitment. Perhaps that's the secret of keeping 'alive'—jump from one medium to another."

—Gloria DeHaven in a 1954 interview discussing the advantages of rotating film work with her nightclub appearances

Dolores Del Rio

Dolores del Rio

(1905–1983)
Actress

Born in Mexico, Dolores del Rio came to America in the 1920s. She took advantage of her exotic looks and became an actress in the mid-1920s. Del Rio starred in the films, *What Price Glory* (1926) and *Flying Down to Rio* (1933).

> *"I suppose it is a very funny thing, but I am happier when I am sad than when everything is so pleasant. If I can cry and cry and cry I am so very, very happy. I have a feeling of tremendous exultation, of being swept on to heights and down into depths which just being glad never gives me."*

—Dolores del Rio

John
Derek
Value
of card:
$10-12

The acting career of John Derek has been over
shadowed by his marriages to four beautiful actresses.
Their names were Pati Behrs, Ursula Andress, Linda
Evans, and Bo Derek. The actor played the part of
Joshua in the 1956 film, *The Ten Commandments*.
Derek died in 1998 while still married to Bo Derek.

*"[John] is a lovely human being. We are very
good friends. Suddenly there was just a divorce between us."*
—Actress Ursula Andress commenting on
John Derek in 1972

Marlene Dietrich

(1901–1992)
Actress

Marlene
Dietrich
Value
of card:
$10-12

Marlene Dietrich was a star in European films before coming to Hollywood to act. The German-born actress starred in the films, *The Blue Angel* (1932) and *Witness for the Prosecution* (1957). Dietrich was rarely seen in public toward the end of her life.

> *"All the time I was in Berlin Garbo was my favorite. I only had Sunday afternoons free; I was playing, rehearsing, all the other time. So on Sunday afternoons I used to go to see Garbo's pictures. I followed them from one theater to another; maybe sometimes I saw one five or six times. And when I came to America I thought perhaps I will meet her. I hear she likes German people. But now, no. She would think, 'Humph, she is just someone else trying to be like me.' I cannot blame her, but it was cruel of people to say such things."*

—Marlene Dietrich commenting in 1930 on people referring to her as the second Greta Garbo, the actress

Troy Donahue

(1936–2001)
Actor

Troy
Donahue
Value
of card:
$10-12

TROY DONAHUE.

Troy Donahue became an actor and pop figure.
His heyday in films was the late 1950s and early 1960s.
The boyish-looking Donahue co-starred with actress
Sandra Dee in the 1959 film, *A Summer Place*.

> *"I've been lucky all the way, even like my new
> name which is a better professional tag than my own
> name, Merle Johnson. My mother and sister loved it
> from the start and never call me anything but Troy."*
> —Troy Donahue, 1960

Kirk
Douglas
Value of
card: $5-7

"Footprint Ceremony"
Grauman's Chinese Theatre

Kirk
Douglas
Value of
card: $5-7

Kirk Douglas

(1916–)
Actor

The cleft chin of Kirk Douglas became his facial trademark of sorts that he used to his advantage in Hollywood. His acting roles in films were often tough-guy characters. But Douglas starred in movies that required a more soft touch such as *Lust for Life* (1956).

"Some of my best friends are actors."
—Kirk Douglas

Melvyn Douglas

(1901–1981)
Actor

Melvyn Douglas
Value
of card:
$10-12

Melvyn Douglas won Oscars and critical acclaim as an actor. The Georgia-born Douglas got his start in films in the early 1930s. *The Americanization of Emily* (1964) and *Hud* (1963) are a few of his many film works.

> *"On the other side of the coin, I run into a lot of young people who talk about being actors, but who actually want to be celebrities. I run into a lot more of them now than in my younger days. There is a tremendous desire on their part to be a celebrity in some field or another. But you can be a celebrity by just winning a beauty contest. That doesn't make you an actor."*
> —Melvyn Douglas, 1964

Billie Dove - Lloyd Hughes

Billie Dove

Billie Dove and
Lloyd Hughes
Value of card:
$10-12

Billie Dove

(1903–1997)
Actress

Billie
Dove
Value
of card:
$10-12

Billie Dove appeared on stage in the Ziegfeld Follies as a teenager. The actress had a brief film career
with most of it confined to the 1920s. Dove starred
in the films, *Wanderer of the Wasteland* (1924) and *The
Black Pirate* (1926).

*"I don't like talking pictures very much so far. I
believe most people are going to prefer the silent drama
after the novelty wears off. Aside from that, I should
start in where most of us have to, and they say my
voice is quite all right. They gave me a surprise test,
you know—three men came to see me. They seemed
strangely silent and watchful and encouraged me to do
most of the talking—and it was not until afterwards
that I learned they had been making a Firnatone test
of my voice. I'm glad they didn't tell me, I might have
been self-conscious. Anyway the verdict was good. So
if I do make some talking pictures, I shall probably be
all right."* —Billie Dove, 1928

Irene Dunne

(1898–1990)
Actress

Hollywood actress Irene Dunne was equally at home playing in comedies, dramas, and musicals. The 1931 film, *Cimarron*, earned her an Academy Award nomination. Dunne starred in the films, *The Awful Truth* (1936) and *My Favorite Wife* (1940).

"Actors and actresses don't always know what is best for them. When they think they do, it is usually the beginning of the end."
—Irene Dunne

Deanna Durbin, Nan Grey, Helen Parrish, and Charles Winninger
Value of card: $10-12

DEANNA DURBIN

UNIVERSAL

Deanna Durbin
Value of card:
$7-9

Deanna Durbin

(1921–)
Actress

Deanna Durbin was born in Canada in 1921. The actress had starring roles in the films, *Mad About Music* (1938) and *It Started with Eve* (1941). She retired from the screen in the late 1940s. Today, Durbin is an elusive target for those seeking an interview.

"I was never happy making pictures. They never allowed me to grow up as a normal child."
—Deanna Durbin, who became a huge star in her early teens, commenting on her film career in 1958

64 54/1

Sally Eilers

„Ross" Verlag

Reproduction verboten

Sally
Eilers
Value
of card:
$10-12

Sally Eilers

(1908–1978)
Actress

Sally Eilers started her film acting during the last years of the silent era. She played the role of Grace Martin in the film, *Slightly Used* (1927). But sound pictures would be where Eilers became a star. She starred in the films, *A Holy Terror* (1931) and *Disorderly Conduct* (1932).

> *"I'm going to devote all of my time to pictures and forget about marriage. It's too easy to get a reputation in Hollywood of being engaged too often."*
> —Sally Eilers after announcing in 1929 that her wedding engagement was off

JULIAN ELTINGE
IN THE
"FASCINATING
WIDOW"

Julian Eltinge

(1881–1941)
Actor

Julian
Eltinge
Value of
card: $7-9

Born in Massachusetts, Julian Eltinge was a man who made his living playing a female on stage and screen. He is possibly the most famous of all female impersonators the world has known. Eltinge's film work included the film, *The Clever Mrs. Carfax* (1917). But it was the stage where Eltinge did most of his acting.

> *"I would resent a man's impersonating a woman myself. I only decided to perfect the damn thing so well because I discovered there was a mint of money in it!"*
>
> —Julian Eltinge, a female impersonator

Fabian

Fabian
Value
of card:
$10-12

Fabian
Value of card:
$10-12

Fabian

(1942–)
Singer

Fabian was a pop singer that started turning out hit records in the 1950s. One of his records was called "Tiger" (1959). Ultimately he did not have a good voice and his hit-making days ended soon after they began. Fabian has film and television work to his credit as an actor.

"I hope my singing improves so I can do real songs."
—Fabian, 1959

Douglas Fairbanks

(1883–1939)
Actor

Mary Pickford

(1892–1979)
Actress

The marriage between silent-film actors Douglas Fairbanks and Mary Pickford may be the most famous coupling in Hollywood history. They were both top stars on the screen at the time of their 1920 marriage. One of Pickford's many films was *Rebecca of Sunnybrook Farm* (1917). In 1924, Fairbanks would star in *The Thief of Bagdad* (1924). Fairbanks gave Pickford a Beverly Hills mansion as a wedding gift. The home was called Pickfair. Ultimately the two would divorce, but stayed on friendly terms till the death of Fairbanks in 1939.

> *"From a personal standpoint I have found that having a husband who is an optimist brings great happiness. Douglas Fairbanks talks continually of happiness, health, and success, never of their opposites. He apparently can see nothing else."*
> —Mary Pickford, 1925

Douglas Fairbanks, Jr.

(1909–2000)
Actor

Actor Douglas Fairbanks, Jr. was the son of Douglas Fairbanks, a legendary silent-film actor. In 1929, Fairbanks, Jr. married a lady who would become a film legend, actress Joan Crawford. He starred in the films, *Little Caesar* (1930) and *Gunga Din* (1939). The marriage between Fairbanks, Jr. and Crawford ended in 1933.

> *"I have never cared about keeping up with the Joneses. But I used to have small-talk arguments about how the Rolls-Royce is the cheapest car to buy because it lasts so long. It's sometimes an economy to get good things."*
> —Douglas Fairbanks, Jr.

Charles Farrell

(1901–1990)
Actor

Charles Farrell

„Iris"-Verlag

Charles Farrell was paired with actress Janet Gaynor in the late 1920s in films. The pairing made the actor a Hollywood star. *The Man Who Came Back* (1931) was one of the films Farrell starred in with Gaynor. Farrell also is famous for television's "My Little Margie" which ran in the 1950s.

> *"I'm so sorry to learn that you tell dirty stories, but I like you, anyway."*
> —From a female fan letter sent to Charles Farrell in the mid-1920s

Charles Farrell Value of card: $10-12

Alice Faye

(1915–1998)
Actress

Alice Faye
Value of
card: $4-6

Alice Faye started her entertainment career as a singer. Faye became a Hollywood actress in the 1930s doing such films as *Poor Little Rich Girl* (1936), a musical with actress Shirley Temple. She worked with actor Tyrone Power in the film, *In Old Chicago* (1937). Faye was described by a friend as someone not being aware of how famous she was with the public.

"I know that I have an inferiority complex, but I can't do anything about it. It probably started when I first came out [to Hollywood]. I know that the studio didn't voluntarily ask for me. It was at Rudy Vallee's request that I was given a small part in George White's Sandals. It was an accident that threw me into the lead after I got here. My ensuing pictures were not what one might call startling successes.

"I didn't believe that anything would come of it then. I still longed, as I had from the start, for my contract to end so that I could return to New York. Now you couldn't drag me away from Hollywood."
—Alice Faye, 1937

Errol Flynn

(1909–1959)
Actor

Errol
Flynn
Value of
card: $7-9

Errol Flynn is remembered for both his film acting and his off-screen carousing that included drinking and chasing after women. Actor David Niven knew him well. Niven told of Flynn being dependable for one thing: letting you down. Flynn was a swashbuckler in several films, including *Captain Blood* (1935).

> *"I feel the word adventure was written in his soul. His gallantry was of the spirit, and not just in motion picture scripts."*
> —Producer Jack Warner eulogizing Errol Flynn

Henry
Fonda

(1905–1982)
Actor

Henry FONDA

65.

Henry
Fonda
Value
of card:
$10-12

Henry Fonda acted in many classic films. *The Grapes of Wrath* (1940) and *The Ox-Bow Incident* (1943) are among the films he had starring roles in. Fonda's daughter is actress Jane Fonda. He died in Los Angeles, California, in 1982.

"I was not, shall we say, a go-getter. I guess I was sort of a bum."
—Henry Fonda recalling his younger days after dropping out of college

• Glenn Ford

Foto: Metro-Goldwyn-Mayer   RÜdel-Verlag

Glenn Ford

(1916–2006)
Actor

Glenn Ford once confessed he was amused at how his acting career survived despite so many bad films. He came to fame in the mid-1940s from the roles he played in a couple of 1946 films, *Gilda* and *A Stolen Life*. Ford died in 2006 in Beverly Hills, California, where he lived for many years.

"Glenn Ford decided I should learn to smoke a cigar. I did and threw up. Then he put my cowboy hat under his horse to 'christen' it."
—Actress Shirley MacLaine, who starred with Glenn Ford in the comedy-western film, *The Sheepman* (1958).

Connie Francis

(1938–)
Singer

Connie Francis was a teenager when she signed her first deal to make records. Among the singer's number-one hits is the 1958 song called "Stupid Cupid." Francis's heyday as a hit-record maker was in the late 1950s and early 1960s.

"For a long time, I thought I had to imitate other singers. I hadn't gotten anywhere singing my way. I was afraid to be natural. But then I decided to try once more with 'Who's Sorry Now?' I was relaxed, happy, natural, and that was the way it come through, for my first gold record."
—Connie Francis

Clark Gable

(1901–1960)
Actor

Clark Gable will always be remembered for playing the role of Rhett Butler in the film, *Gone with the Wind* (1939). Early in his acting days, Gable didn't think his good luck in Hollywood would last. But Gable's fame was no fluke as he became one of the most famous stars in the world.

> *"When I was young, M-G-M was a very exciting place to be. I've always loved movie stars, loved movies, loved everything about them except doing them. It was so tremendously thrilling to go into the commissary for lunch. They were all there—Judy Garland, Lana Turner, Spencer Tracy, Hedy Lamarr. And there was the lovely, sweet smell of the pancake make-up the women wore—so much more exciting than the grease paint they use now. Every time Clark Gable walked in I just about dropped my fork."*
> —Actress Elizabeth Taylor

Greta Garbo

"Ross" Verlag

Reproduction verboten

Greta Garbo — Lew Ayres

Greta Garbo
(1905–1990)
Actress

Greta Garbo started her movie career in Europe where she was born. The actress began making Hollywood movies in the mid-1920s. Garbo played opposite actor John Gilbert in *Flesh and the Devil* (1926) and it made her a star. Off screen, Garbo and Gilbert would have a famous romance. Garbo could be eccentric at times. She loved walking in the rain. In 1931, a reporter caught her sitting atop the fence of a horse corral at sunset. "I like to smell horses and look at sunsets," Garbo explained to the reporter.

"Garbo had an icy look in her eyes when anyone sought to impose upon her, as, according to studio gossip, Groucho Marx discovered one day. He saw a well-known figure approaching in slacks and floppy hat, waylaid her, bent down in his famous crouch, and peeked up under the brim. Two prisms of pure Baltic blue stared down at him, and he backed away, muttering, 'Pardon me, ma'am. I thought you were a guy I knew in Pittsburgh.'"
—Actor David Niven

Ava Gardner
(1922–1990)
Actress

AVA GARDNER

Ava Gardner Value of card: $10-12

Actress Ava Gardner starred in films with famous stars and married famous entertainers. She starred with actor Clark Gable in the 1953 film, *Mogambo*. Gardner married actor Mickey Rooney, bandleader Artie Shaw, and singer Frank Sinatra.

> *"The truth is that the only time I'm happy is when I'm doing absolutely nothing. I don't understand people who like to work and talk about it like it was some sort of goddamn duty. Doing nothing feels like floating on warm water to me. Delightful, perfect."*
> —Ava Gardner

Janet Gaynor

Janet Gaynor

Janet Gaynor
Value of card:
$10-12

Janet
Gaynor
Value
of card:
$10-12

Janet Gaynor

(1906–1984)
Actress

Janet Gaynor was an actress in both silent and talking pictures. *Sunrise* (1927) and *A Star Is Born* (1937) were films she acted in during her career. Gaynor won an Oscar for Best Actress in a Leading Role at the first Academy Awards ceremony held in 1929. It was for a collection of films rather than one, as was often the case for the awards presented during the early history of the Oscars. Gaynor died in Palm Springs, California, in 1984.

> *"At that time, the fans wouldn't let you alone, period. Oh, I know, 'Ho, ho, ho—too bad you couldn't walk down the street!' But you couldn't. You could not go anywhere.*
> *"I spent years never seeing anything because I had to sit with my back to the room in a restaurant. And in the days of the silents everybody wanted to touch you because they didn't think you were real."*
> —Janet Gaynor, in 1973, recalling her early film days in the 1920s and 1930s

Mitzi Gaynor

(1931–)
Actress

636

MITZI GAYNOR

Mitzi
Gaynor
Value
of card:
$8-10

Mitzi Gaynor is a singer, dancer, and actress. Her signature film is *South Pacific* (1958). Actors Gene Kelly and Marilyn Monroe are among the stars Gaynor has worked with in films. Gaynor worked with Monroe on a film called *There's No Business Like Show Business* (1954). The entertainer also has done plenty of television specials beginning in the 1960s.

> *"I'm the only one in South Pacific who sang for herself—even Juanita Hall's voice was dubbed. But at the intermission I heard a woman sitting behind me tell her companion: 'Do you know Mitzi Gaynor is the only one in the film who doesn't sing for herself?'"*
> —Mitzi Gaynor

4212/1

Universal phot

Hoot Gibson

Reproduction verboten

„Ross" Verlag

Hoot
Gibson
Value
of card:
$8-10

Hoot Gibson

(1892–1962)
Actor

Cowboy-actor Hoot Gibson was a big star in the silent-film era. *Cavalcade of the West* (1936) was among his memorable sound westerns. The actor was a good horse rider whether the camera was rolling or not. Gibson was not able to save his Hollywood riches and struggled to make ends meet late in life.

> "*I don't believe any influence has been greater that of the western pictures in bringing to the public throughout the country an intimate knowledge of the country between the Mississippi and the Pacific Coast.*"
> —Hoot Gibson, 1927

JOHN GILBERT

John Gilbert — Greta Garbo

John Gilbert

(1897–1936)
Actor

John Gilbert was a major silent-film actor. He starred in the hugely successful film, *The Big Parade* (1925). He entered life as an unwanted baby on the part of his mother. Love for Gilbert was difficult as an adult as well. Gilbert would go through four wives and four divorces.

> *"I have been on the screen for twenty years and I have managed to squeeze out of it complete unhappiness. Today I can't get a job. I mean exactly that. I-can't-get-a-job. Four short years ago I had a contract calling for $250,000 a picture. Today I can't get a job for $25 a week or for nothing at all. It doesn't make sense, but there it is."*
> —John Gilbert, 1934

Lillian Gish
Value
of card:
$10-12

Lillian Gish

Verlag „Ross" Berlin SW 68.

(1893–1993)
Actress

Actress Lillian Gish is believed to have the longest screen career in Hollywood history. She may also have been the loveliest actress to ever appear on screen. One of her first films was the 1912 silent, *The Painted Lady*. The last picture Gish starred in was released in 1987. It was called *The Whales of August*. Gish virtually dedicated her life to her acting. She did almost everything in life to prepare her for more stage or film work. Gish died wealthy in New York in 1993. Her sister was actress Dorothy Gish.

"Stories often came from a casual remark. Dorothy had been with Biograph while I was working with David Balasco in the theatre. One day the company was discussing the newcomer, me, when Mr. Griffith overheard Lionel Barrymore say that I looked as if I couldn't kill a cockroach. D.W. wrote a story around such a character, changing the roach to a mouse, and called it 'The Lady and the Mouse.'"

—Lillian Gish recalling her early days in silent films

Paulette Goddard

(1910–1990)
Actress

Actress Paulette Goddard became a celebrity in the early 1930s due to her dating actor Charles Chaplin. Goddard was used by Chaplin in his 1936 film, *Modern Times*. The two actors would marry in the mid-1930s, but were divorced by the early 1940s. Goddard starred in another of Chaplin's film called *The Great Dictator* (1940). Goddard's heyday in films was the decade of the 1940s.

> *"Paulette struck me as being somewhat of a gamine."*
> —Actor Charles Chaplin

Paulette
Goddard
Value
of card:
$10-12

Betty Grable
(1916–1973)
Actress

Betty
Grable
Value
of card:
$10-12

Today, Betty Grable is best remembered as a pin-up girl during World War II. Her Hollywood acting is less remembered. Grable had success in musical comedies. Two of her films were *Down Argentine Way* (1940) and *Coney Island* (1943).

"Hollywood has a way of letting you down that is rather discouraging. I guess the only reason I'm in a Broadway show is that the films don't want me. It comes like something of a shock after you've worked in several studios and have been publicized around the country for years, suddenly to realize there are no new roles for you."

—Betty Grable commenting on her film career in circa 1939 during her stage run of the play, *Du Barry was a Lady*

Cary Grant

(1904–1986)
Actor

Cary Grant banked numerous classic films as a Hollywood actor. The actor known for his good looks co-starred in *The Philadelphia Story* (1940) with actress Katharine Hepburn. Off screen, Grant was said to be a difficult person to be around. The leading man managed his finances well and would die worth tens of millions of dollars.

> *"The woman who talks baby talk. She's gotta go!"*
> —Cary Grant

JEAN HARLOW   METRO-GOLDWYN-MAYER

Jean Harlow

(1911–1937)
Actress

Actress Jean Harlow became a Hollywood sensation in the 1930s. *Red Dust* (1932) and *Dinner at Eight* (1933) are among the films she starred in. A platinum blonde, Harlow married screenwriter Paul Bern in 1932. He committed suicide soon afterward. Harlow was only twenty-six years of age when she died in 1937.

> *"The most important development for a girl ambitious for a screen career, is development of the mind. She should be interested in music. She should read fine books, learn to dance, and possibly, study for one of the sciences."*
> —Jean Harlow, 1936

Mildred Harris Chaplin

Mildred Harris

(1901–1944)
Actress

Mildred Harris (aka Mildred Harris Chapin) Value of card: $13-15

Enerst
B. C. & A. H.
202

Mildred Harris was an actress from the silent-film era. The Wyoming-born Harris would have been long forgotten had she not married comic-actor Charles Chaplin. The two wed in 1918. Harris starred in the film, *Polly of the Storm Country* (1920). She died in 1944.

> *"I have the distinction of never having been one of Mr. Chaplin's leading ladies. I had been a star since I was ten years of age . . . But I never worked with Mr. Chaplin in any of his pictures. It is a little embarrassing when stories get around that Mr. Chaplin engineered your career, when in reality you were a star before he met you."*
>
> —Mildred Harris, the first wife of actor Charles Chaplin, talking to a reporter in 1943, more than two decades after the couple divorced

WILLIAM HART

854

TRIANGLE - FILM

William S. Hart

(1864–1946)
Actor

William
S. Hart
Value
of card:
$7-9

William S. Hart was a popular cowboy actor during the silent-film era. He started his film career at a relatively late age. Hart was in his forties when he first appeared in films. The actor starred in the western-themed film, *Branding Broadway* (1918). Hart died in Newhall, California, in 1946.

"I'll be 64 in December. And yet the other day the Sheriff's station here asked me to take part in shooting practice, and when I showed them some fast and fancy shooting I figured I'd have to apologize for missing the mark so much. I didn't, though. I still can make those babies talk."
—William S. Hart talking to a reporter in 1936

Lillian Harvey

(1906–1968)
Actress

Born in the United Kingdom, Lillian Harvey would start her film acting in silent pictures in Germany. Harvey and actor Willy Fritsch became a popular romantic-screen pairing in European films. But the actress had success without Fritsch in the 1931 film, *The Congress Dances*, made in Germany.

> *"For three years, I was the most popular player in Europe; in all those different countries of Europe. If I appealed to such diverse audiences there, I surely must have something to give to America! My fan mail proves that."*
> —Lillian Harvey speaking in 1934 of her desire to find success in Hollywood

Lillian Harvey — Willy Fritsch

"Ross" Verlag

Reproduction verboten

Lillian Harvey and Willy Fritsch Value of card: $10-12

Willy Fritsch

(1901–1973)
Actor

Born in Poland, actor Willy Fritsch is remembered for playing opposite actress Lillian Harvey in pictures. One of their works was a film made in Germany called *Three from the Gasoline Station* (informal English translated title), released in 1930. The two were thought to be a romantic couple off screen. Fritsch would use his singing voice while acting with the arrival of talking pictures.

Sessue Hayakawa

OFFICIN:
A. B. FILMS, STOCKHOLM.

1059
FÖRLAG NORDISK KONST STOCKHOLM

Sessue Hayakawa
(1889–1973)
Actor

Sessue
Hayakawa
Value
of card:
$8-10

Actor Sessue Hayakawa became the first major Asian Hollywood star. Before he worked in Hollywood, Hayakawa did stage work in Japan, his country of birth. The actor starred in the film, *The Cheat* (1915).

> *"This part, this Col. Saito, this is the first part in all the acting I do that the expression is true for me—it twists my intestines."*
> —Sessue Hayakawa telling of the difficulty in playing Col. Saito in the 1957 film, *The Bridge on the River Kwai*

Helen Hayes

(1900–1993)
Actress

HELEN HAYES

Helen Hayes did so much television work late in her career that her stage and Hollywood career have been less remembered than should be the case, today. The actress starred in the films, *Farewell to Arms* (1932) and *Night Flight* (1933). Hayes bought a mansion in the 1930s located in Nyack, New York. The home was called Pretty Penny.

> *"I can't stand the guilty feeling of taking life easy. Yes, I could play for a season in New York—my farm is only 20 miles away—and then relax, but I not only become bored but down right ill."*
> —Helen Hayes, 1945

Helen
Hayes
Value
of card:
$10-12

Susan Hayward

(1917–1975)
Actress

Susan
Hayward
Value
of card:
$10-12

Born in New York, actress Susan Hayward started her film career in the late 1930s. She starred for Paramount Pictures in the film, *Beau Geste* (1939). Hayward worked with actors Ray Milland, John Wayne, and Paulette Goddard in the 1942 film, *Reap the Wild Wind*. Hayward died in 1975.

> *"Emotions of natural redheads are close to the surface. Film acting requires a girl to produce any one of a dozen emotions before the cameras without preliminary build-up, so the redhead has an immediate advantage."*
> —Susan Hayward, a natural redhead

Rita Hayworth

(1918–1987)
Actress

Today, Rita Hayworth is remembered as a sex symbol of the past. There is no denying she was sexy. But the silver screen offered proof she could act. Hayworth would gain recognition from playing the role of Judith "Judy" MacPherson in the film, *Only Angels Have Wings* (1939). She starred in the 1941 film called *The Strawberry Blonde*. Alzheimer's disease would strike Hayworth. She died in 1987.

"She's the only beagle in the world who behaves like a poodle."
        —Rita Hayworth referring to her dog, Sweetie, during a 1960 interview

Rita Hayworth Value of card: $10-12

William Holden
(1918–1981)
Actor

Handsome William Holden splashed on to the silver screen in the late 1930s. The actor co-starred with actress Barbara Stanwyck in the 1939 film, *Golden Boy*. In 1976, Holden starred in *Network*. Holden died in 1981 after tripping on a rug in his home and hitting his head on a table.

"The day I need make-up I will quit filming."
—William Holden

Camilla Horn

(1903–1996)
Actress

Camilla Horn — John Barrymore

„Ross" Verlag

Reproduction verboten

Camilla Horn and John Barrymore Value of card: $10-12

Beautiful Camilla Horn was a European actress. She began her film acting in her home country of Germany during the early 1920s. Horn would do a couple of Hollywood films with actor John Barrymore. The two actors played opposite each other in *Tempest* (1928) and *Eternal Love* (1929). Horn died in Germany in 1996.

> *"I had to find a girl, pretty, winsome and a good actress, whom the breath of publicity had not yet touched. I found this fragile creature in Miss Horn."*
> —Director F.W. Murnau explaining how he plucked Camilla Horn out of obscurity to star in the 1926 film, *Faust*

Foto: Universal Film, Inc.

Rock Hudson

Rock Hudson

(1925–1985)
Actor

Handsome and chiseled-looking actor Rock Hudson starred with actress Elizabeth Taylor in the film, *Giant* (1956). By the 1970s, Hudson was working on a successful television series called "McMillan & Wife" (1971–1977). The series co-starred actress Susan Saint James as Hudson's wife. Hudson was briefly married in the mid-1950s.

"Even as a little kid I wanted to be a movie star. What made up my mind was seeing Jon Hall do that high dive in '[The] Hurricane' to rescue Dorothy Lamour. I was a swimmer, and at that time I was sure I had scales instead of skin.

"Years later I was skindiving with Paul Stader, the stuntman, and I told him this story. He said, 'Why that was me, not Hall.' I said, 'So you're the one responsible for getting me into this whole crazy thing.'"
—Rock Hudson, 1967

Rock
Hudson
Value
of card:
$10-12

Benita Hume — Merle Oberon — Douglas Fairbanks — Joan Gard

Benita Hume
(1906–1967)
Actress

London-born Benita Hume had an acting career mostly confined to the 1920s and 1930s. *Tarzan Escapes* (1936) with Johnny Weissmuller was one of Hume's last films.

Douglas Fairbanks
(1883–1939)
Actor

Douglas Fairbanks was a famous silent-film actor. He used his athletic talents in his films performing physically challenging feats. Fairbanks starred in *The Thief of Bagdad* (1924) and *Robin Hood* (1922). His marriage to silent-star Mary Pickford is still celebrated, today.

Merle Oberon

(1911–1979)
Actress

Merle Oberon was born and raised in India. In the late 1920s, she traveled to England to become a cabaret singer. Producer Samuel Goldwyn brought Oberon to America and she became a Hollywood star in the 1930s. Among her most memorable films was *Wuthering Heights* (1939).

> *"I really look so different off the screen that at a recent luncheon, a certain prominent Hollywood actress who sat next to me, didn't recognize me and all through luncheon accepted me as a girl apparently trying to break into pictures and gave me words of advice and of warning. But when someone told her my name was Merle Oberon, she became embarrassed and flustered and finally blurted out: 'You, Merle Oberon? I didn't expect to see a tiny young British girl! I expected to see a modern Theda Bara, no less!'"*
> —Merle Oberon, 1935

Joan Gardner

(1914–1999)
Actress

Born in England, Joan Gardner became a Hollywood actress in the 1930s. She teamed with actors Douglas Fairbanks, Merle Oberon, and Benita Hume in the film, *The Private Life of Don Juan* (1934). Gardner died in Beverly Hills, California, in 1999.

Al Jolson — Davey Lee

Al Jolson

(1886–1950)
Entertainer

All the entertainment accomplishments of Al Jolson—and there were plenty—will forever be overshadowed by his acting and singing in the 1927 movie, *The Jazz Singer*. The movie is known as the world's first talkie. Jolson died in San Francisco, California, in 1950 after suffering a heart attack.

> *"Maybe show business is getting to be a lost art. It used to be if a kid was a hit at the theater when they had 'amateur night,' a scout would see him and get him a break in burlesque, or in a medicine show, or the circus. Then if he had what it took he'd latch on in vaudeville. Finally maybe he'd be ready for Broadway in a musical for Ziegfeld or the Shuberts.*
>
> *"But today you don't have that. Radio? A guy smooching in front of a mike, afraid to take his eyes off the script. Phooey! That's not show business."*
> —Al Jolson, 1949

Jennifer Jones

(1919–)
Actress

Born in Oklahoma, actress Jennifer Jones became a Hollywood star with the release of the film, *The Song of Bernadette* (1943). In the movie she played Bernadette Soubirous. The role landed Jones an Oscar for Best Actress in a Leading Role. Jones married producer David O. Selznick in the late 1940s.

"Actually, I never felt I would succeed on the screen. This I must face, I'm not the greatest beauty in the world."
—Jennifer Jones

Buster Keaton

(1895–1966)
Actor

166

Buster
Keaton
Value
of card:
$15-17

At the mere mention of his name, a Buster Keaton fan is likely to start chuckling. Keaton was a comic genius in the silent-film era. *Go West* (1925) and *The Cameraman* (1928) were among his classic films. The actor used his athletic abilities to create physical humor in movies. Less studied is the photogenic face of Keaton. It has been said that Keaton's face may have been the most beautiful to ever appear on screen.

> *"In the silent days we could try anything at all, and did."*
> —Buster Keaton

Ruby Keeler

(1909–1993)
Actress

FILM STARS AND THEIR PETS.
7113 F.
RUBY KEELER

Ruby
Keeler
Value
of card:
$10-12

Actress Ruby Keeler was born in Canada in 1909. She danced on the Broadway stage before turning to acting in Hollywood musicals. Keeler starred opposite actor Dick Powell in *Flirtation Walk* (1934). Her film career is all but confined to the 1930s. Keeler is best remembered today for being married to entertainer Al Jolson for a little over a decade, beginning in 1929.

"Fame, success—it's so fleeting. And even when you're at the top you have many moments alone without that audience."
—Ruby Keeler

Grace Kelly
(1929–1982)
Actress

Grace
Kelly
and
Frank
Sinatra
Value
of card:
$12-14

Grace Kelly en Frank Sinatra

IN M.G.M's HIGH SOCIETY

Grace Kelly became a princess without having to kiss a frog. The actress married Prince Rainier III of Monaco in 1956. Kelly was a Hollywood star before her celebrated marriage. She starred in such films as *Mogambo* (1953) and *Rear Window* (1954).

"I don't want to dress up a picture with just my face. If anybody starts using me as scenery, I'll do something about it."
—Grace Kelly, 1955

20th CENTURY FOX

Deborah Kerr
(1921–2007)
Actress

Deborah
Kerr
Value
of card:
$8-10

Born in the Scotland, Deborah Kerr acted in film productions made in the United Kingdom before coming to Hollywood. She would star in the MGM film called *The Hucksters* (1947). Kerr was nominated for an Oscar as Best Actress in a Leading Role for her part in *Separate Tables* (1958).

"Let's not limit it to Hollywood—it's this country of yours with such friendly people—they've brought me out. Losing my shyness has made me what is laughingly called 'blossom.'"
—Deborah Kerr on what Hollywood has given her that she most values

Alan Ladd

(1913–1964)
Actor

Alan Ladd made his mark as an actor in the 1953 film, *Shane*. In the film, Ladd plays ex-gunslinger Shane who shoots it out with bad-guy Jack Wilson, played by actor Jack Palance. Ladd was married to actress Sue Carol for over two decades beginning in the early 1940s. The marriage ended with Ladd's death in 1964.

"I'm not worried when [my fans] ask me for autographs. I'll worry when they quit asking."
—Alan Ladd

A 2289/2
„Ross" Verlag
Dorothy Lamour
Reproduction verboten

Dorothy Lamour

(1914–1996)
Actress

Actress Dorothy Lamour will forever be remembered as co-starring with actors Bob Hope and Bing Crosby in several "Road" movies. *Road to Morocco* (1942) and *Road to Utopia* (1946) were among the trio's famous films. Lamour married twice in her lifetime.

"I don't mind—I love it, in fact. I'll make all the sarong-native girl-tropical moonlight pictures that are offered."
—Dorothy Lamour, 1952

Dorothy Lamour Value of card: $10-12

Burt Lancaster

(1913–1994)
Actor

Burt Lancaster became a film star after his first film, *The Killers* (1946). Prior to films, he worked as a circus acrobat. Lancaster would star as a former, great trapeze artist in the 1956 film, *Trapeze*. He played the lead role in *Jim Thorpe: All American* (1951).

> "There are times when I want to get out of the business. Everybody wants to make these big epic entertainments. They're empty. And worst of all, a lot of them just aren't very well made, but the critics go overboard.
>
> "The thing is that everybody obviously wants deeply to laugh at anything today. It's like the war years in that people want escapism, big escapism. What the devil, it's a nervous world we live in. But it's the affluent society, too, and we're all on a spending spree. The bigger the picture, the bigger the ticket, the better."
> —Burt Lancaster, 1965

Rod Laroque

„Iris"-Verlag

Films Erka

ROD LA ROCQUE

192

Rod La Rocque
Value of card:
$7-9

Rod La
Rocque
Value of
card: $7-9

Rod La Rocque

(1898–1969)
Actor

Rod La Rocque worked on stage as an actor before taking his talents to the silent screen. He would star in the movie, *The Ten Commandments* (1923). La Rocque married silent-film actress Vilma Banky in 1927. Their marriage lasted until La Rocque's death in 1969.

"Marriage is a business. I have a lot of work to do. You can't succeed in two businesses at once."
—Rod La Rocque, 1924

JERRY LEWIS

PHOTO PARAMOUNT

727

Jerry Lewis

(1926–)
Comedian/Actor

Jerry
Lewis
Value
of card:
$8-10

Comedian Jerry Lewis teamed with singer Dean Martin and they became one of the most celebrated comedy acts in entertainment history. The duo was a hit on film and in nightclubs. Lewis would have a falling out with Martin and split with him in the mid-1950s. On his own, Lewis would act and star in the films, *The Nutty Professor* (1963) and *King of Comedy* (1983).

"Work never killed anyone, it's the pressure that's bumping people off. Regardless of who I'm talking with, if I become uncomfortable I walk away, spit twice, take a deep breath and count to sixty. It took two of the finest specialists in the world to teach me that."
—Jerry Lewis

Harold Lloyd

(1893–1971)
Actor

Harold Lloyd Value of card: $6-8

Harold Lloyd was a comic star during the silent-film era. *Safety Last* (1923) and *Girl Shy* (1924) are among the films he starred in. He did film work in the 1930s and one film in the 1940s, but his best work belonged to the 1920s. Lloyd was worth millions of dollars when in died in 1971.

> *"You see, so many comedies are constructed on trouble, difficulties that you have to get into, and it's overcoming these difficulties that allows you to succeed. Here's the difference. My character, when I put on glasses, was able to look more like the normal boy you met on the street. The romance was believable. I could win the girl."*
> —Harold Lloyd

Gina Lollobrigida

(1927–)
Actress

Gina Lollobrigida used her luscious looks to her advantage in films. The actress began her film work in her home country of Italy. But she would work in Hollywood beginning in the 1950s. Lollobrigida starred with actors Burt Lancaster and Tony Curtis in the 1956 film, *Trapeze*.

"As soon as I decided to make acting my career I saw every movie I could. I would go back again and again, and I learned from the mistakes of the bad actors as well as from my favorites, Bette Davis, Katharine Hepburn and Lilli Palmer."
—Gina Lollobrigida

Carole Lombard

(1908–1942)
Actress

Carole Lombard

„Ross" Verlag

A1150/1

Reproduction verboten

Carole Lombard is known for acting, marrying actor Clark Gable, and dying tragically in a plane crash in 1942. She was married to Gable and only thirty-three years old at the time of her death. One of Lombard's films was *My Man Godfrey* (1936).

"I can't resist pets and I can't walk by a pet shop."
—Carole Lombard

Foto: Michalke/Ufa

Sophia Loren

Sophia Loren

(1934–)
Actress

Known for her beauty, actress Sophia Loren was born in Rome, Italy. Loren gained Hollywood's attention after appearing in some Italian movies such as *The Miller's Beautiful Wife* (1955). She came to America to make films in the mid-1950s. Loren starred along side actors Cary Grant and Frank Sinatra in a film called *The Pride and the Passion* (1957).

> *"Do you know that the pizza in southern Italy is the dish of the poor? I come to America and see pizza signs everywhere. So I think America not so rich after all. Then I find eating pizza here is like eating hot dog—it's for fun."*
> —Sophia Loren

Bessie Love

(1934–1986)
Actress

Bessie Love has a name that may sound familiar to the casual film fan of today, but few would know why. The Texas-born Love was a silent-film star. The actress starred with actor Douglas Fairbanks in *Reggie Mixes In* (1916). Love's Hollywood career stalled in the mid-1930s when she moved to Britain.

> *"Would you be kind enough to print that I am not dead? I have many friends out home and they might be hurt to think I had not let them know."*
>
> —Bessie Love, writing from England in 1967, to the *Los Angeles Times* who had mistakenly listed her as passed away in a then-recent article

Bessie
Love
Value
of card:
$12-15

121

Ida Lupino

(1914–1995)
Actress

London-born actress Ida Lupino made many for-gettable movies in her career. *Ready of Love* (1934) and *Paris in Spring* (1935) were among such productions. Lupino co-starred with actor Humphrey Bogart in the 1941 film, *High Sierra*. For many years, begin-ning in the 1950s, Lupino would turn to television for work.

> *"I've never really liked acting. It's a tortuous pro-fession and it plays havoc with your private life. You have to keep thinking of your face. If, for instance, your husband would like to go out for an evening, you can't join him. You have to consider how you'll look the next day if you don't get the proper amount of sleep."*
> —Ida Lupino

Jeanette MacDonald

(1903–1965)
Actress

Jeanette MacDonald was a singer on stage before she sang in pictures. The actress was keep busy in the 1930s by MGM with such films as *Naughty Marietta* (1935) and *San Francisco* (1936). The Philadelphia-born MacDonald had a movie career lasting just two decades. Her film career closed with the 1940s. MacDonald married actor Gene Raymond in the late 1930s. The Hollywood couple stayed together until MacDonald's death in 1965.

"Friends ask me to sing at parties, but I feel silly standing up and being prima donna-ish."
—Jeanette MacDonald, 1936

Shirley MacLaine
(1934–)
Actress

Shirley MacLaine has prospered through decades of film acting that began in the mid-1950s. She starred with actors Anthony Perkins and Shirley Booth in the 1958 film, *The Matchmaker*. The Virginia-born actress would go on to star in such classics films as *The Apartment* (1960) and *Terms of Endearment* (1983). MacLaine's brother is actor Warren Beatty.

Jack Lemmon
(1925–2001)
Actor

Jack Lemmon had success as an actor with such classic films as *Some Like It Hot* (1959) and *The Apartment* (1960). Born in Newton, Massachusetts in 1925, Lemmon first went in front of a camera in the late 1940s, doing mainly television work. Off screen, he was described as down-to-earth and friendly. Lemmon graduated from Harvard University and served his country in the Navy.

> *"Jack Lemmon, my darling Jack, is the epitome of what it means to be a nice person. He was always prepared, yet mischievously open for a good laugh. His genius was so riveting that I would often come in on my days off or stay late at night just to watch him cast his comic spell before the camera."*
> —Actress Shirley MacLaine, who starred with Jack Lemmon in *The Apartment* (1960) and *Irma La Douce* (1963)

Shirley
MacLaine
and Jack
Lemmon
Value of
card: $4-6

Fred MacMurray

(1908–1991)
Actor

Fred Mac-
Murray
Value of
card: $7-9

Today, Fred MacMurray is unfairly remembered by only a couple of accomplishments in front of the camera. The actor co-starred with actress Barbara Stanwyck in the classic film-noir, *Double Indemnity* (1944). MacMurray had success with the television show called "My Three Sons" (1960–1972).

> *"You're making a mistake. I can't play that. It requires acting."*
> —Fred MacMurray responding to director Billy Wilder who offered him a co-starring role in *Double Indemnity* (1944)

Fredric March

(1897–1975)
Actor

FREDRIC MARCH   PARAMOUNT PICTURES

Fredric March was born in Wisconsin in 1897 and began film acting in the silent-movie era of the 1920s. His classic films include *A Star Is Born* (1937) and *The Best Years of Our Lives* (1946). During the heyday of the Hollywood studio system, March avoided long-term studio-employment contacts. Off screen, when it came to a mate the actor did enjoy being tied to someone for the long term. March stayed married to actress Florence Eldridge for decades, until his passing in 1975.

Fredric March Value of card: $6-8

> *"My argument in defense of make-up stems to 1932 when I won an Academy Award for Dr. Jekyll and Mr. Hyde. At that time I, too, was a young leading man. I accepted the role because it afforded me the opportunity to do something besides smile and make love to lovely leading ladies."*
> —Fredric March

127

Herbert Marshall

(1890–1966)
Actor

HERBERT MARSHALL   PARAMOUN

London-born Herbert Marshall acted in Broadway plays in the 1920s. He appeared in the 1925 play called *These Charming People*. But starting in the late 1920s he made films in Hollywood. In 1929 Marshall acted in the drama film called *The Letter* (1929). He starred in *Trouble in Paradise* (1932) with actresses Miriam Hopkins and Kay Francis. Less known is that Marshall lost a leg after sustaining an injury in World War I.

> *"When I was beginning I played butlers, soldiers, counts, sailors, the forelegs of a horse and even a coat rack."*
> —Herbert Marshall

Tony Martin

(1912–)
Singer/Actor

Cyd Charisse

(1921– 2008)
Actress

Singer Tony Martin and dancer Cyd Charisse have been a couple for decades. The two married in 1948. Martin sang in the musical film, *Ziegfeld Girl* (1941). Charisse would dance on film with actor Fred Astaire in *The Band Wagon* (1953). Martin has made many nightclub appearances as a singer during his long entertainment career. Martin and Charisse have lived in the Palm Springs, California area for decades.

"Cyd and I were working together on a picture and she walked as if she were on a cloud. When I talked with her I felt sweetness and tenderness, qualities more important than beauty, but she didn't like me at first."
—Tony Martin on meeting his wife Cyd Charisse

Virginia Mayo Value of card: $10-12

Virginia Mayo
(1920–2005)
Actress

Virginia Mayo had sexy legs coupled with facial beauty to offer Hollywood. The actress starred with actor Bob Hope in the comedy film called *The Princess and the Pirate* (1944). Prior to working in films, Mayo worked on the Broadway stage. She died in Thousand Oaks, California in 2005.

"[It] happened on the first flight of Howard Hughes' Constellation to New York. My idol had always been Walter Pidgeon, and I found myself sitting beside him on the plane. Halfway to New York, I got airsick. Pidgeon was so kind—he even held a wet hanky on my forehead. But I was mortified. Every time I see that man I try to hide."

—Virginia Mayo telling columnist Hedda Hopper, in 1954, of her most embarrassing moment

Victor McLaglen

(1886–1959)
Actor

Victor Mc Laglen

Born in Britain, Victor McLaglen was a prize-fighter before he turned to film acting. He appeared in silent films in Britain before finding his way to Hollywood. McLaglen won an Oscar for Best Actor in a Leading Role for his part in the John Ford-directed film, *The Informer* (1935).

Victor McLaglen Value of card: $5-7

> *"The thing that pleased me most in getting the award was the telephone message of congratulation I received from my brother Kenneth in England. He talked to me for four and a half minutes, which proved to me he was in the money."*
> —Victor McLaglen on winning an Oscar in 1936

131

Glenn Miller

(1904–1944)
Bandleader/
Musician

Glen Miller

COURTESY OF
GEORGE B. EVANS

A MUTOSCOPE CARD
MADE IN THE U.S.A.

Glenn
Miller
Value
of card:
$5-7

Glenn Miller was a hugely successful bandleader beginning in the 1930s. He sold many recordings such as "Sunrise Serenade" (1939). Today, Miller's name is still easily recognized beyond just music circles. Miller died serving in World War II as a band leader for the Army.

> *"All of us orchestra leaders must develop a style of our own. When people tune in on the air they want to be able to recognize the different bands. So just as a classical-music enthusiast can distinguish Toscanini from Stokowski and Barbirolli from Ormandy, so the jazz lover knows the difference between Dorsey and Goodman or Duchin. Any one can recognize my band, because of its unusual use of the saxophones and the accent given to the harmonic structure."*
> —Glenn Miller, 1941

Patsy Ruth Miller

(1904–1995)
Actress

4220/1   Universal phot.

Patsy Ruth Miller

„Ross" Verlag   Reproduction verboten

Patsy Ruth Miller came to stardom on film in the early 1920s. The Missouri-born actress starred in the films, *Camille* (1921) and *The Hunchback of Notre Dame* (1923). She played opposite actor Lon Chaney in the later film. During her career she would act with cowboy-stars Tom Mix and Hoot Gibson. Miller was friends with actor Rudolph Valentino.

> *"Please excuse me today. I'm just recovering from a slight attack of Long Beach. It's a wonder I haven't rheumatism and gray hair after staying there so long. Never, oh never, have I seen such a lot of old people. I have to be with young folks or I die."*
> —Patsy Ruth Miller commenting in 1924 on Long Beach, California, where she was staying during the filming of *Head Winds* (1925)

133

Carmen Miranda and Tom Breneman

Carmen Miranda

(1909–1955)
Singer/Actress

Born in Portugal and raised in Brazil, actress Carmen Miranda is best remember today for having fruit piled atop her head. Her fanciful and varied hats were plenty in number during her entertainment career. Miranda did radio and movie work in Brazil before coming to America. She became a star in Hollywood musicals in the early 1940s. *Week-End in Havana* (1941) and *Babes on Broadway* (1941), were among the films Miranda starred in early in her Tinseltown days. She died of a heart attack at the age of forty-six.

> *"I am too busy to get married. There have been five proposals from fine men, including a doctor and a lawyer, but I am not ready to think of marriage yet. There is one thing very certain—I will not choose an actor!"*
> —Carmen Miranda, 1946

Robert Mitchum

(1917–1997)
Actor

Bob Mitchum

Actor Robert Mitchum was both tough on screen and in life. He did time on an honor farm after being busted for marijuana possession in the late 1940s. "It's just like Palm Springs without the riffraff," Mitchum said of his incarceration. The Connecticut-born Mitchum starred in the films, *Cape Fear* (1962) and *Farewell, My Lovely* (1975).

"But there's one wonderful thing about this business. You're privileged to meet some great people. There's a bond of sincere commiseration. The stuffed shirts form a fence behind which the others can get and tell naughty stories."
—Robert Mitchum on the business of acting

Robert
Mitchum
Value
of card:
$10-12

TOM MIX and TONY.

Tom Mix
Value
of card:
$8-10

Tom Mix

(1880–1940)
Actor

Tom Mix was one of the biggest stars of western-themed films made in the silent-movie era. Mix appeared in over three-hundred films during his Hollywood career. Tony, Mix's horse, was the cowboy actor's sidekick. One of his early movies was called *Ranch Life in the Great Southwest* (1910). He starred in the 1925 film, *Riders of the Purple Sage*. Mix did more than act. He also wrote and produced many of his films. Mix was famous for his high living which included moving into a Beverly Hills, California, mansion in the 1920s.

"There are horses, and there are just animals, but the finest bit of horseflesh I have ever thrown a leg over is Tony, the horse I ride now in my pictures."
—Tom Mix, 1922

Metro Goldwyn Mayer 475

Robert Montgomery and Tallulah Bankhead
Value of card: $10-12

Robert Montgomery

(1904–1981)
Actor

Born in New York, Robert Montgomery started his film-acting career with some 1929 films. In 1931 he appeared opposite actress Norma Shearer in the film called *Private Lives*. The pairing made him a Hollywood star. Montgomery would star in the 1941 film, *Mr. and Mrs. Smith*. He would gain further fame in the 1950s from his television series, "Robert Montgomery Presents."

Tallulah Bankhead

(1902–1968)
Actress

Tallulah Bankhead had a last name that was easy to remember. The actress had a first name that might be difficult to spell by memory. Bankhead was born in Huntsville, Alabama, in 1902. She began acting as a teenager. Her first film role in Hollywood was in the late 1920s. Bankhead's most memorable film acting was done in the Alfred Hitchcock-directed classic, *Lifeboat* (1944).

"Of course, I'd like to make a good picture . . . But I'd rather die than make another bad picture."
—Tallulah Bankhead, 1936

137

Colleen Moore

Colleen Moore

Colleen
Moore
Value
of card:
$13-15

Colleen Moore
Value of card:
$13-15

Colleen Moore

(1900–1988)
Actress

Colleen Moore was born in Port Huron, Michigan in 1900. As a child, Moore would dream of becoming a film star. As a teenager she would begin to fulfill her wish. Among the early films Moore acted in were *An Old Fashioned Young Man* (1917) and *Hands Up!* (1917). *Flaming Youth* (1923) and *Lilac Time* (1928) are some of her more memorable movies. Today, Moore remains in the memory of the public due mainly from photos of her still being displayed in magazines.

> *"College girls everywhere cut their hair in Dutch bobs. They copied my clothes. No longer did a girl have to be beautiful to be sought after. Any plain Jane could become a flapper. No wonder they grabbed me to their hearts and made me a movie idol."*

—Colleen Moore on the impact of her starring role in *Flaming Youth* (1923)

RITA MORENO   20th CENTURY FOX

D 778

Rita Moreno

(1931–)
Actress

Rita
Moreno
Value
of card:
$8-10

Rita Moreno was born in Puerto Rico in 1931. The actress is best known for her role as Anita in the film, *West Side Story* (1961). But she had been acting in film and television for years prior. In 1971, Moreno acted the part of Louise in the film, *Carnal Knowledge*. Television work has always keep Moreno busy over the years.

> *"For the first time in my life I can not only afford to say no—but even when I can't afford to I can still say it. This is due to West Side Story. It's probably the first film I've ever done—and I've done something like 17 in 14 years out here—where I can agree with someone who says it's great."*
> —Rita Moreno, 1961

Alla Nazimova

(1879–1945)
Actress

Actress Alla Nazimova was born in Russia in 1879. She began her acting on a stage in Moscow at the Artistic Theater. A violin player as a child, Nazimova came to America after the turn of the century to continue her stage work. She would eventually make her debut as a film actress on the silent screen. *Camille* (1921) and *Salome* (1923) are among her better-known films. Late in her career she would drop her first name and go by just her last name, Nazimova. At the height of her fame, Nazimova had a mansion on Sunset Boulevard in what is now the city of West Hollywood, California. The house no longer stands.

> *"I lived there once, in that poorest part of Whitechapel. So poor we were, we Russian players, that, while we dazzled rich sophisticated London by night, we had to live and board in the poorest London by day."*
> —Alla Nazimova

Patricia Neal

(1926–)
Actress

Patricia Neal is an attractive actress whose film work includes *The Fountainhead* (1949). She would win an Oscar for Best Actress in a Leading Role for her work in the film classic, *Hud* (1963). Born in Kentucky, Neal got her start in acting on the stage.

> *"I didn't think I had too many friends left in Hollywood. Gossip about Gary [Cooper] and me was being whispered all over town. No official Cooper separation had been declared and no one wanted to be on the wrong side when the lines were finally drawn. I was no longer the young darling of Hollywood."*
> —Patricia Neal on her plight in 1951 due to the fallout from her affair with actor Gary Cooper

Patricia
Neal
Value
of card:
$10-12

Pola Negri

5468

„Iris"-Verlag

Pola
Negri
Value
of card:
$10-12

Pola Negri

Verlag „Ross" Berlin SW 68.

Pola Negri

(1897–1987)
Actress

Born in Poland, Pola Negri was a silent-film actress who starred in *Passion* (1919) and *Forbidden Paradise* (1924). Besides her film work, she was known for her off-screen melodramatic behavior and romances. Negri dated actors Rudolph Valentino and Charles Chaplin.

"When the ship stopped at Ellis Island the American press swarmed aboard. It was my first experience with them. I was accustomed to interviews in Europe where one question is submitted at a time. It was different here. This pushing, shouting, asking a thousand questions at once, absolutely threw me into a panic. In my confusion I momentarily forgot every word of English I knew."
—Pola Negri on arriving in the U.S. in the early 1920s

Ozzie Nelson

COURTESY OF
MUSIC CORPORATION OF AMERICA

A MUTOSCOPE CARD

Ozzie
Nelson
Value
of card:
$6-8

Ozzie Nelson

(1906–1975)
Actor

Actor Ozzie Nelson played a family man on the television show, "The Adventures of Ozzie and Harriet" (1952–1966). Nelson's wife in the series was played by actress Harriet Hilliard, his off-screen wife.

"Two generations ago, a boy knew just a few girls, all in his own town—after he'd called on her three times, his intentions were questioned. Today's young people have hundreds of friends, possibly all over the country. They like variety (we've found that on our TV show) and can have it—three dates in a row doesn't mean anything permanent."
—Ozzie Nelson, 1957

DAVID NIVEN AND GINGER ROGERS

R.K.O. RADIO

David
Niven
and
Ginger
Rogers
Value
of card:
$10-12

David Niven

(1910–1983)
Actor

London-born actor David Niven was a natty dresser in films and a witty talker, off screen. He was a brave man as well. Niven was one of the first stars to serve his country when World War II broke out in 1939. He served in the British army. His films included *Dodsworth* (1936), *Separate Tables* (1958), and *The Pink Panther* (1963). Niven died in Switzerland in 1983.

> *"To be an actor, it is essential to be an egomaniac; otherwise it just doesn't work."*
> —David Niven

KIM NOVAK

Kim Novak

(1933–)
Actress

Kim Novak burst onto the movie screen in the mid-1950s. She had done modeling work before becoming a film star. The Blonde-bombshell actress starred opposite actor William Holden in the 1955 film, *Picnic*. Novak's other films include *The Man With the Golden Arm* (1955) and *Strangers When We Meet* (1960). In the late 1950s, a story had spread through Hollywood speaking of a possible romance between Novak and singer Sammy Davis, Jr.

> *"The more I work, the more I can take. But I guess I couldn't keep this pace the rest of my life. And I pull my own strings, no matter what you read about the studio setting out deliberately to mold a new star to replace Rita Hayworth. If they were going to do that, they'd have dyed my hair red."*
> —Kim Novak, 1957

Merle Oberon

(1911–1979)
Actress

Born in India, actress Merle Oberon was brought to Hollywood by producer Samuel Goldwyn in the mid-1930s. She had gained attention from her film work in the United Kingdom. Oberon starred with actor Fredric March in the film, *The Dark Angel* (1935). She is famous for her role as Cathy Linton in the 1939 film, *Wuthering Heights*. Oberon died in Malibu, California in 1979.

"Because I'm a resident of England, Britannia taxes my Hollywood income as well. I bought a house at Regent's Park so I pay property taxes on that, too. My agent gets 10 percent, incidentals account for another 10 percent and living expenses for 25 percent. So there's always a deficit. No wonder Charles Laughton, Robert Donat, Leslie Howard don't come to Hollywood any more."
—Merle Oberon, 1938

147

Gloria
Noble and
Donald
O'Connor
Value of
card: $6-8

Donald O'Connor
(1925–2003)
Actor

Donald O'Connor danced and sang in films. The actor starred in the musical film called *Get Help to Love* in 1941. O'Connor played the role of Peter Sterling in the comedy, *Francis* (1950). His most memorable role was Cosmo Brown in the film, *Singin' in the Rain* (1952).

> *"One night I was dog tired after an unusually tough day. I had to get my mind off work. A good western picture might do the trick I thought. So I went straight to the theater to see Apache and walked across the street when that was finished and took in Broken Lance. Then had a bite to eat and drove home and slept like a baby."*
> —Donald O'Connor, 1954

Maureen O'Sullivan

(1911–1998)
Actress

MAUREEN O'SULLIVAN.   Metro-Goldwyn-Mayer.

No 81.

Maureen O'Sullivan was born in Ireland in 1911. The actress was discovered by director Frank Borzage who spotted her at a horse show in Dublin. O'Sullivan would make it to Hollywood and play the role of Jane in many "Tarzan" movies. She is the mother of actress Mia Farrow. O'Sullivan died in Arizona in 1998.

"Dirt somewhere in the house is not as important as being gentle and understanding when your child needs you."
—Maureen O'Sullivan

Maureen
O'Sullivan
Value
of card:
$10-12

Gregory Peck

(1916–2003)
Actor

Gregory Peck Value of card: $8-10

Born in La Jolla, California, actor Gregory Peck starred in many classic films during his Hollywood career that began in the mid-1940s. Among his early films were *The Yearling* (1946) and *Gentleman's Agreement* (1947). Peck's acting career was helped by his good looks and tall frame. Off screen, he was active in political and humanitarian causes. Peck died in Los Angeles, California, in 2003.

"If anybody was least likely to succeed, Greg was definitely it. He would be the last person I would've thought would make it."
—Richard Lustig, a classmate of Gregory Peck's at San Diego High School

Anthony Perkins

(1932–1992)
Actor

Born in New York, Anthony Perkins entire acting career is buried under his most famous role, Norman Bates. Perkins played Bates—a motel operator who is crazy—in the film, *Psycho* (1960). The actor died in California in 1992.

Anthony Perkins Value of card: $10-12

> "Paris is terribly expensive and I don't see how anyone would do a picture here for reasons of economy. It must be something else. Perhaps it's what the French call 'ambiance.'"
> —Anthony Perkins while on location in Paris filming *Glaive et la balance, Le* in 1962

Millie Perkins

(1938–)
Actress

Actress Millie Perkins starred as Anne Frank in the 1958 movie called *The Diary of Anne Frank*. It was her first film job and remains her most famous. Perkins was a model prior to working in Hollywood. Besides films, Perkins has done plenty of television.

"Many young people would like to be under contract. But Fox didn't understand me. You know what they'd say? 'We see a great career ahead of you. We're going to put you in a great film.' But I wasn't asking for that. All I asked was to have a little experience. I spent 2 ½ years arguing with them."
—Millie Perkins, 1961

MARY PICKFORD

Mary Pickford

(1892–1979)
Actress

Mary Pickford became one of the most-famous silent-film actresses in the world. She would earn millions of dollars from her screen work. As a child, Pickford was raised by her mother under conditions of extreme poverty. *Rebecca of Sunnybrook Farm* (1917) and *Sparrows* (1926) were famous films of the actress who became known to the public as "America's Sweetheart." Besides her movie work, Pickford is famous for her marriage to actor Douglas Fairbanks in 1920.

Mary Pickford Value of card: $7-9

> *"Well, I remember when I used to go into managers' offices to apply for jobs. I always was afraid I'd be either too short or too tall for the role I was applying for. So I used to scrooch down as little as I could, so that if they said I was too small I could suddenly grow up right there before their eyes."*
> —Mary Pickford commenting on how she would land roles as a young and not-yet-famous actress

W.704　　　　DICK POWELL　　　　COLUMBIA

Dick Powell

(1904–1963)
Actor

Dick
Powell
Value of
card: $6-8

Dick Powell earned money as a singer before being paid as an actor. Powell joined up with actress Joan Blondell in films and the two starred in musicals such as *Stage Struck* (1936). Powell would join Blondell in marriage in 1936. The couple's marriage did not have a "Hollywood" ending. Powell and Blondell divorced in the mid-1940s.

> *"I want a home, a wife and children—and no competitive career stuff. For that matter, I cannot see how any girl would willingly marry anyone in the show business. I'm not going to, unless she'll quit."*
>
> —Dick Powell, who went on to marry actresses Joan Blondell and June Allyson, speaking in 1934

William Powell

(1892–1984)
Actor

William
Powell
Value of
card: $6-8

William Powell acted in over ninety films and enjoyed over ninety years of life. Born in Pennsylvania in 1892, Powell started acting in films in the early 1920s. His early films included *Outcast* (1923) and *The Bright Shawl* (1923). He is most famous as the leading man opposite actress Myrna Loy in the film, *The Thin Man* (1934), and its sequels. Powell is also remembered for his off-screen romance with actress Jean Harlow. The actor married and divorced actress Carole Lombard in the 1930s.

> *"I am really a very fine worrier. I worry about almost anything. I worry about all my picture roles. But I do all my serious worrying away from the studio. For instance, I have a nice swimming pool. I worry about it being a waste of space in the back yard."*
> —William Powell, 1934

Tyrone Power

Tyrone Power

(1914–1958)
Actor

Tyrone Power was keep busy as a leading-man actor playing romantic parts. His father was silent-film actor Tyrone Power, Sr. The actor's movies include *In Old Chicago* (1937) and *Witness for the Prosecution* (1956). Power was married to actresses Annabella and Linda Christian.

> *"Anybody who isn't happy in America wouldn't even be happy in heaven."*
> —Tyrone Power

Debbie Reynolds

(1932–)
Actress

Debbie Reynolds got Hollywood's attention after winning a beauty contest in the late 1940s. The actress danced on film with actor Gene Kelly in the musical, *Singin' in the Rain* (1952). Reynolds starred in another musical called *The Unsinkable Molly Brown* (1964). The 1996 comedy called *Mother* is among her more recent film work.

Debbie
Reynolds
Value
of card:
$8-10

> "I find that the working side of this business, going to work, working on scripts is the easiest part. The difficult part is the nonprivacy.
>
> "Every breath that you take is known, even before you perform it. I'm sure that if you were in the same position there are many things you do that you would not want to share with everyone."
>
> —Debbie Reynolds, 1960

Charles Rogers

4680/1

„Ross" Verlag

Reproduction verboten

Charles "Buddy" Rogers

(1904–1999)
Actor

Charles
"Buddy"
Rogers
Value
of card:
$10-12

Charles "Buddy" Rogers had success as a silent actor with films such as *Wings* (1927). But today he would perhaps be a faint Hollywood memory without his marriage to silent-star Mary Pickford in 1937. Earlier, the two had starred together in the 1927 film, *My Best Girl*. Rogers and Pickford adopted two children early in their marriage. But the kids would live out their adulthood estranged from their famous parents.

> *"I came out of Kansas into Hollywood and movie people were my gods. I was very awed by them. Maybe that's why I didn't get places with my picture work, why I let the studio keep on putting me in kid roles. I'm not awed any more, thank heaven. I haven't been very far away—just New York—but at least I have learned there are other people to know and other things to see. It was time I learned it. I am getting old. I am nearly 30."*
> —Charles "Buddy" Rogers, 1932

Ginger Rogers

(1911–1995)
Actress

Actress Ginger Rogers gained fame by taking actor Fred Astaire on as a dancing partner in films starting in the early 1930s. *Flying Down to Rio* (1933) was the first film they danced in, together. Rogers would also star in *Swing Time* (1936) and *Kitty Foyle: The Natural History of a Woman* (1940). Her success as an actress allowed Rogers to build a mansion just inside Beverly Hills, California, during the late 1930s. The home included a soda fountain.

Ginger Rogers Value of card: $10-12

"Those pictures I made with Fred Astaire still hold up on today's TV and all types of people praise them. They were made for sheer entertainment, fun, and yes, we had fun making them—though, in those days before the Screen Actors Guild, we'd sometimes work through the nights, two days at a time. And at the end of those long stretches, that's when they would do close ups of me."
—Ginger Rogers, 1971

MICKEY ROONEY   METRO-GOLDWYN-MAYER

Mickey Rooney

(1920–)
Actor

Born in New York, actor Mickey Rooney began his screen work as a child star in the 1920s. Prior to that, he was used in the vaudeville act of his parents. Rooney is short in stature and during his prime his hair was slicked-backed and wavy. Beginning with the film, *A Family Affair* (1937), Rooney took to playing the role of Andy Hardy with great success. He starred in *National Velvet* in 1944 with actress Elizabeth Taylor. Rooney has had many ups-and-downs in both fame and fortune during his long career. His first of many wives was actress Ava Gardner. They had a brief marriage in the early 1940s.

> *"And with the exception of Mickey, I've never had a husband or boyfriend who was a good dancer."*
> —Actress Ava Gardner speaking in 1990 of her ex-husband Mickey Rooney

Barbara Rush

(1927–)
Actress

Barbara Rush made her acting debut on a theater stage as a child. As an adult, Rush would act in the films, *Magnificent Obsession* (1954) and *Bigger than Life* (1956). She played the wife of actor Kirk Douglas in the 1960 film, *Strangers When We Met*. Rush has done a lot of television work in her career.

Barbara Rush Value of card: $10-12

"A studio feels that if it can't make a star out of you it doesn't want to continue trying to build you up. This was a blow that made me take stock of myself. I felt that others with no more to their appearance and ability than I had were getting ahead. I realized what I lacked was confidence. My mother is terribly shy and both my sister and I have subconsciously copied her. This had to go, I told myself."
—Barbara Rush, 1957

Rosalind Russell

(1907–1976)
Actress

Rosalind Russell was a graduate of the American Academy of Dramatic Arts. She would act on Broadway and get her Hollywood start in the 1930s. Her screen career got moving after she starred in *Craig's Wife* (1936). Russell starred with actresses Norma Shearer and Joan Crawford in the film, *The Women* (1939).

"My first time on [film] was with Myrna Loy and Bill Powell in 'Evelyn Prentice' and a man with a black glass kept getting in my way. I asked Bill why he didn't keep out of our path. 'He's the cameraman,' Bill said."
—Rosalind Russell, 1965

Tommy Sands

(1937–)
Singer

Teen idol Tommy Sands had his first hit song as a singer in 1957 with "Teenage Crush." Besides getting his singing career off the ground in the 1950s, Sands started acting as well. He starred in the films, *Sing Boy Sing* (1958) and *Mardi Gras* (1958). Sands did admit to not hanging on to the money he earned during the first burst of his entertainment career. After his marriage to singer Nancy Sinatra ended in 1965, Sands went to Hawaii and "lived on the beaches and bummed around for several years."

Tommy Sands Value of card: $10-12

"Suddenly at 18, overnight, I was a star. The next four years were probably the most miserable in my life. I wasn't prepared. I always wanted to be an actor. When I die I want to leave something. Suddenly, I wasn't doing what I wanted to do. I was a rock 'n' roll singer."
—Tommy Sands, 1964

163

Maria Schell

(1926–2005)
Actress

Maria Schell was born in Austria in 1926. She would begin her career in film acting in Europe. *The Magic Box* (1951) was one of Schell's European films. But she would do Hollywood films. Schell starred opposite actor Yul Brynner in the film, *The Brothers Karamazov* (1958).

"I've fallen in love with America. Your habit of eating steak, tomatoes, and chilled grapefruit; this concentration Americans have on eating only the right foods for beauty and figure intrigues me. I thought little about that in Europe. I worried only over my acting ability there. But here I am thought pretty and everything must be done to enhance the idea. It does something nice to my ego, as every actress likes to be thought pretty."
—Maria Schell, 1957

Maria
Schell
and Yul
Brynner
Value
of card:
$10-12

Maria Schell - Yul Brynner

Yul Brynner

(1915–1985)
Actor

Actor Yul Brynner will be forever tied to the play and film he did called *The King and I*. He first did the stage production in the early 1950s and the film version in 1956. Brynner was known for his bald head and unique looks.

"All young actors dream of success, but it's a bitter kind of thing for man—you lose the most valuable thing in the world, privacy."
—Yul Brynner

LIZABETH SCOTT

356

MAL WALLIS

Lizabeth
Scott

Lizabeth Scott

(1922–)
Actress

Lizabeth
Scott
Value
of card:
$10-12

Lizabeth Scott began appearing in movies during the 1940s. The beautiful actress used her blond hair and husky voice to carry her in such films as *Dead Reckoning* (1947) with actor Humphrey Bogart. But Scott never became a big star. She acted along side other famous actors besides Bogart. Among them were Kirk Douglas, Herbert Marshall, and Elvis Presley. By the late 1950s her movie career was over though she did appear in a 1972 film called *Pulp*.

> *"At school I used to be teased about two things— dyeing my eyebrows and my husky voice. They used to say to me, 'Where did you get those eyebrows?' or 'Where did you get that voice?' I didn't know whether it was good or bad."*
> —Lizabeth Scott

Omar Sharif

(1932–)
Actor

OMAR SKARIF

Born in Egypt, actor Omar Sharif is best known for his role as Dr. Yuri Zhivago in the film, *Doctor Zhivago* (1965). He also co-starred with actress Barbra Streisand in the 1968 film, *Funny Girl*. Sharif married Egyptian actress Faten Hamama in the 1950s. They couple divorced in the 1970s.

Omar Sharif
Value
of card:
$10-12

"Zhivago was an awful part to play. I couldn't go to the daily rushes and see myself do that one big, good scene that would have gotten me into gear. I started eating my heart out, and I had a sort of breakdown after one month. I said, 'David, you made a mistake in picking me,' but he replied, 'Trust me,' and I kept on going."

—Omar Sharif, on working with director David Lean on the 1965 film, *Doctor Zhivago*

167

Norma Shearer
(1902–1983)
Actress

Norma Shearer was a leading-lady actress in many MGM films. In 1927, she married Irving Thalberg who was one of the studio's top executives. Shearer starred in *The Divorcee* (1930) for MGM. Her role in the film gained the actress an Oscar for Best Actress in a Leading Role. Thalberg had a history of fragile health and he died in 1936 at the age of thirty-seven. Shearer would have a long and happy second marriage beginning in 1942.

"I'm scared of comedy. I think it demands stage experience and I've never been before the footlights. I wish I had. Do you know, I have a curious recurrent dream that I am in a stage play and most embarrassed— like those dreams when one is caught in extreme negligee in some public place."
—Norma Shearer, 1933

Dinah Shore

(1916–1994)
Singer

Tennessee-born singer Dinah Shore recorded many hit records beginning in the 1940s. "Dear Hearts and Gentle People" (1949) was a hit record of Shore's. Earlier, Shore had worked with singer Frank Sinatra before either of them had launched their professional entertainment careers. Today, she is best remembered for her television show called "The Dinah Shore Show" (1951–1957). Shore married actor George Montgomery in the 1940s. The couple would divorce in the 1960s.

> *"I like people."*
> —Dinah Shore

Dinah Shore Value of card: $6-8

Frank Sinatra
(1915–1998)
Singer

Frank Sinatra captured the ears of the world with his unique singing talent. One of his most remembered songs is "My Way" (1968). Sinatra was so popular of an entertainment figure that he was often called "The Chairman of the Board." Besides voice talents, he also had acting ability. Sinatra won an Oscar for Best Actor in a Supporting Role for his part in the 1953 film, *From Here to Eternity*. The singer knew the type of girls he liked to date. "I like an intelligent woman," Sinatra told an interviewer in 1965.

"A singer like [Sinatra] comes along once in a lifetime. Why did it have to be my lifetime?"
—Singer Bing Crosby

Barbara Stanwyck

(1907–1990)
Actress

Barbara Stanwyck was an orphan in her childhood. She was a movie star as an adult. Stanwyck's signature movie was the 1944 film, *Double Indemnity*. But the Brooklyn-born Stanwyck is perhaps best remembered for her work on television's "The Big Valley." The series ran for some years in the 1960s.

"I would hate to do it all over again. Life is a pretty difficult thing."
—Barbara Stanwyck at seventy years of age

Barbara Stanwyck Value of card: $10-12

James Stewart

(1908–1997)
Actor

James
Stewart
Value
of card:
$8-10

Classic films come to mind when one thinks of the Hollywood career of actor James Stewart. He did a lot of them. Among such Stewart films are *Mr. Smith Goes to Washington* (1939), *It's a Wonderful Life* (1946), and *Vertigo* (1958). Stewart's best-known film characters were steadfast when facing challenging situations. The actor was raised in Indiana, Pennsylvania. During adulthood, his film earnings allowed him to live in a mansion. Comedian Jack Benny was both a neighbor and close friend of Stewart while he lived in Beverly Hills, California.

"There are down-beat, dirty pictures. They deal with futility and hopelessness. The hell with 'em. I'm not going to make them."
—James Stewart, 1961

Gloria Swanson

GLORIA SWANSON

162

Gloria Swanson
Value of card:
$10-12

Gloria Swanson

(1897–1983)
Actress

Gloria
Swanson
Value
of card:
$13-15

Silent-screen star Gloria Swanson is best re-membered for playing a former silent-screen star in the 1950 film, *Sunset Boulevard*. This does not seem fair given the many film accomplishments of the Chicago-born actress. Swanson first gained fame and fortune in silent films such as *Sadie Thompson* (1928). When riches came to her early in her movie career she bought a so-called "dream palace" in Beverly Hills, California. Swanson believed a star should live like a star. Actor Tab Hunter met the actress. Hunter described Swanson as being physically "tiny."

> *"With the arrival of talking pictures, everyone in the world was suddenly conscious of accents. The funny part was that most of the men with all the money in Hollywood, from Joe Kennedy to Adolph Zuckor, had heavy accents themselves and many of them could neither detect a phony accent nor verify an authentic one."*
> —Gloria Swanson

173

Norma Talmadge

(1893–1957)
Actress

Norma
Talmadge
Value
of card:
$10-12

Norma Talmadge became a silent star with such films as *Smilin' Through* (1922) and *Camille* (1927). The actress married producer Joe Schenck in 1916. Talmadge divorced Schenck in 1934. The same year, she married another producer, George Jessel. Talmadge's marriage to Jessel did not make it out of the 1930s. She had famous sisters in actresses Natalie Talmadge, the first wife of actor Buster Keaton, and Constance Talmadge.

"It isn't inspiration that makes moving picture stars—It's downright hard work."
—Norma Talmadge, 1923

Elizabeth Taylor

(1932–)
Actress

As a kid, actress Elizabeth Taylor starred in the film, *National Velvet* (1944). As an adult, the actress, known for her beauty and famous marriages, starred in *Giant* (1956) and *Cat on a Hot Tin Roof* (1958). To the public, Taylor is much more than a famous actress. She is a huge public personality.

> *"The first day I saw Richard Burton on the 'Cleopatra' set, there was a lot of hemming and hawing, and he said hello to Joe Mankiewicz and everyone. And then he sort of sidled over to me and said, 'Has anybody ever told you that you're a very pretty girl?' And I said to myself, Oy gevaldt, here's the great lover, the great wit, the great intellectual of Wales, and he comes out with a line like that. I couldn't believe it. I couldn't wait to go back to the dressing room where all the girls were and tell them."*
> —Elizabeth Taylor

Elizabeth Taylor Value of card: $12-14

ROBERT TAYLOR AND HEDY LAMARR

Robert
Taylor
and Hedy
Lamarr
Value
of card:
$10-12

Robert Taylor

(1911–1969)
Actor

Blue-eyed actor Robert Taylor became wealthy working the oftentimes-despised Hollywood studio system during his career. MGM employed him for over twenty years starting in the 1930s. He starred in the 1942 film called *Johnny Eager*. The good-looking Taylor married actress Barbara Stanwyck in 1939. The Hollywood couple divorced in 1951.

> *"I know this thing might just be a flash in the pan. Don't know, but for some reason my look caught on, but that can't carry you far."*
> —Robert Taylor after MGM put him under contract in 1935

Hedy Lamarr

(1914–2000)
Actress

Actress Hedy Lamarr used her beauty in films such as *Tortilla Flat* (1942) and *Samson and Delilah* (1949). Some critics were harsh on her acting ability. Some said her beauty was the only thing she brought to films. Strangely, the actress was arrested for shoplifting in the mid-1960s. The alleged crime took place just outside the city limits of Beverly Hills, California. Lamarr would beat the charge.

> *"[Louis B. Mayer] wanted me to sign at once but I thought we should both think it over. Then I heard they were sailing for America. I booked passage on the same boat, and had only enough money to keep me for a month in Hollywood if my hopes went wrong."*
> —Hedy Lamarr on meeting producer Louis B. Mayer in London

TRO-GOLDWYN-MAYER

SPENCER TRACY AND FREDDIE BARTHOLOMEW

METRO-GOLDWYN-M

Spencer Tracy and Freddie Bartho-lomew Value of card: $10-12

Spencer Tracy

(1900–1967)
Actor

Spencer Tracy is known to Hollywood fans for making many classic films. A close second to his film ledger in their memory might be his off-screen, long-term romance to actress Katherine Hepburn. The two actors were tangled together romantically while Tracy remained married to his only wife, Louise. Among the films he made were *Boy's Town* (1938) and *Guess Who's Coming to Dinner* (1967). Tracy died in 1967.

> *"I worried that I'd look like a dope when they curled my hair for the part of Manuel, and it didn't help any when Joan Crawford yelled from her car on the lot one day, 'Hey, look who's here. It's Harpo Marx.'"*
> —Spencer Tracy on his role in *Captains Courageous* (1937)

Rudolph Valentino

Rudolph
Valentino
Value
of card:
$10-12

Rudolph Valentino

(1895–1926)
Actor

Rudolph Valentino is perhaps the best-known romantic leading-man actor of silent films. He had guts when it came to trying to land Hollywood acting gigs. Valentino once approached a famous producer and asked for work. Another time he walked up to the world's then-most famous actress, Mary Pickford, and asked for her for advice on breaking into movie business. But Valentino would hit film stardom in the early 1920s. His breakout movie was *The Four Horsemen of the Apocalypse* (1921). Death cut short Valentino's career in 1926 at the age of thirty-one.

> *"One can live a simple life in Hollywood, despite reports to the contrary. You can be out in the open. You can ride horseback and even go swimming in the winter. New York has its decided advantages—plays, operas, art exhibits, auctions—and I would not want to stay away from it too long. But frankly, I would rather work in Hollywood."*
>
> —Rudolph Valentino

253 · R. VALENTINO

Rudolph
Valentino
Value
of card:
$10-12

Rudolph Valentino — Nita Naldi

Nita Naldi

(1897–1961)
Actress

Born in New York, Nita Naldi was a successful stage actress before gaining success in Hollywood. She acted in the 1920 film called *Dr. Jekyll and Mr. Hyde*. Naldi starred with actor Rudolph Valentino in the films, *Blood and Sand* (1922) and *A Sainted Devil* (1924). Naldi's Hollywood career was over with the advent of sound movies.

"Silent screen sirens had one thing in common, we were all blind as bats. Theda Bara couldn't see a foot ahead of her and poor Rudy [Valentino] groped his way through many a love scene, and I really mean groped... [The studios] all used big reflectors to get extra light from the sun. It was so blinding we all had to squint—that's how we acquired that interesting Oriental look."
—Nita Naldi

Mamie Van Doren
(1931–)
Actress

Born in South Dakota, Mamie Van Doren is an actress and sex symbol. She won beauty contests as a teenager. In the early 1950s, she caught the attention of RKO studio mogul Howard Hughes who put her in some of his pictures. Van Doren would star in *Ain't Misbehavin'* in 1955 for Universal Studios who had earlier signed her to a film contract. By the time the 1960s had arrived, Van Doren was mixing movie work with television appearances. The sexy bombshell has been married five times.

> *"By the time I'd worked for three lawyers, I'd been chased around desks so often I figured I had what it takes for more important endeavors like show business."*
> —Mamie Van Doren

Lupe Velez

(1908–1944)
Actress

Lupe Velez – Rod La Rocque

„Ross" Verlag

Lupe Velez and Rod La Rocque Value of card: $10-12

Mexican-born Lupe Velez splashed into Hollywood in the late 1920s. The actress could play comedy or drama roles. Velez is most known for the series of Mexican Spitfire comedy films that began in 1940 which showcased her exciting screen presence. She starred in *Mexican Spitfire* (1940) and followed it with *Mexican Spitfire Out West* (1940). Velez is famous for her off-screen romance with actor Gary Cooper. She was married to actor and Tarzan star Johnny Weissmuller in the 1930s. Velez took her own life in 1944 inside her home in Beverly Hills, California.

"Love! Pooh! It's the bunk. I, for one, never heard of it."
    —Lupe Velez, 1933

Florence Vidor

"Ross" Verlag

Florence
Vidor

(1895–1977)
Actress

Florence
Vidor
Value
of card:
$7-9

Florence Vidor was a silent-era actress who starred in such films as *The Countess Charming* (1917) and *Alice Adams* (1923). She would work for some early Hollywood studios such as Vitagraph Company of America and Jesse Lasky Feature Play Company. Vidor married director King Vidor in 1915. The marriage did not last past the 1920s.

> *"I used to be full of ideas about matrimony. But now I don't know anything about anything. That is I can't express myself. Either you can live happily with a man or you can't. You see? I put it so poorly."*
> —Florence Vidor, speaking in 1924, following her separation from director King Vidor

W. 622   **RICHARD WIDMARK**   20th CENTURY FOX

Richard Widmark

(1914–2008)
Actor

Richard Widmark is famous for acting in noir films in the late 1940s. His most famous of these is the 1947 film, *Kiss of Death*. Widmark played Tommy Udo in the film and it earned him an Oscar nomination.

> *"If we had a theater here in Beverly Hills, a legitimate theater, things might be different. An actor could go into a play between pictures. He could keep artistically fit through exercise of his talents. We should be more facile than we are—I'm speaking of the movie group. If we had such a theater, I know tourists would flock to it; it would be a show place for film actors and the colony would help support it too."*
> —Richard Widmark, 1953

Esther
Williams
Value
of card:
$10-12

Esther Williams
Value of card:
$10-12

Esther Williams

(1921–)
Actress

Pools, swimming talents, and camera lenses combined to make Esther Williams a famous actress. The teenage swimming champion used her abilities in films referred to as "Aqua Musicals." She swam and acted in films such as *Bathing Beauty* (1944) and *Million Dollar Mermaid* (1952). Williams's acting days were over by the early 1960s.

"The swimming musical presented new challenges in hair, makeup, and costuming. Techniques that worked on dry land didn't work in the pool, and we had to feel our way as we went along."
—Esther Williams

Les Vedettes de Cinéma —
N°25 — LOIS WILSON
film Paramount
AN
PARIS

Lois Wilson

(1894–1988)
Actress

Lois Wilson began her film-acting career in the early days of the silent era. *The Pool of Flame* (1916) and *The Gay Lord Waring* (1916) were among her first films. Wilson would finish her work in front of a camera in the 1950s doing television. Despite appearing in over one-hundred films in her lifetime, Wilson is not well known to film fans of today.

> *"This howl set up against cruelty to animals in picture making is really unnecessary. In making* The Thundering Herd *at Mammoth, Cal., we went without sufficient food and shelter for some time. Many of the actors were badly hurt, but the buffaloes and horses came through without a scratch.*
>
> *"I have seen the cowboys cover their horses with their own bedding in very cold weather. The precious buffaloes used in making the picture were carefully tended.*
>
> *"And after all our hardships, one critic—whom I particularly like to please—gave all of the credit to the horses and cameramen."*

—Lois Wilson, talking with a southern drawl, in 1925

SHELLEY WINTERS

Shelley Winters

(1920–2006)
Actress

Today, Shelley Winters is thought of as an over-weight presence on movie screens. But in her early Hollywood acting years she was a sexy star with a much thinner body. Winters did modeling for the Ladies Garment Workers before acting in films. She starred in the 1972 film, *The Poseidon Adventure*.

"*. . . I took [tennis] lessons faithfully twice a week for six years. When I got married, I brought my young husband, Vittorio Gassman, to the Beverly Hills Tennis Club and, although he had been on the Italian Olympic basketball team, he had never held a tennis racket in his hand. The first time we played, he beat me 6-0. I broke my racket and threw it away, and that was the last time I ever played tennis.*" —Shelley Winters on quitting tennis in the early 1950s

Loretta Young

(1913–2000)
Actress

Loretta Young.

Loretta Young was born in Utah in 1913. Her first credited film role as an actress was in *Sirens of the Sea* (1917). She was Simonetta in the film, *Laugh, Clown, Laugh* (1928), which starred Lon Chaney. Young would play plenty of melodrama roles in her screen career. She passed away in Los Angeles in 2000.

> *"I've already received an Academy Award and made a lot of money for the studios and enough for me, too. Now I want to try television because I can control the product."*
> —Loretta Young talking about the direction of her acting career in the early 1950s

Loretta Young Value of card: $10-12

Selected Bibliography

Fox Charles Donald and Milton L. Silver. *Who's Who on the Screen*. New York City, Ross Publishing Co., 1920. Reprint, New York: Gordon Press, 1976.

Internet Movie Database, Inc. http://www.imdb.com.

Los Angeles Times: Archives, 12/4/1881 – present, http://www.latimes.com/.

Monush, Barry. *The Encyclopedia of Hollywood Film Actors: From the Silent Era to 1965*. New York, NY.: Applause Theatre & Cinema Books, 2003.

Index